In case of loss, please return to:

_____

_____

_____

_____

As a reward: $ _____

MENTOR

HOW ALONG-THE-WAY DISCIPLESHIP WILL CHANGE YOUR LIFE

BY CHUCK LAWLESS

Published by LifeWay Press®
© 2011 LifeWay Press
Reprinted 2014

No part of this work may be reproduced or transmitted in any form or by any means, electronic or mechanical, including photocopying and recording, or by any information storage or retrieval system, except as may be expressly permitted in writing by the publisher. Requests for permission should be addressed in writing to LifeWay Press®, One LifeWay Plaza, Nashville, TN 37234-0152.

ISBN: 978-1-4158-7001-3
Item: 005378213

Dewey Decimal Classification Number: 158
Subject Heading: MENTORING \ CHRISTIAN LIFE \ BIBLE--BIOGRAPHY

Printed in the United States of America.

Young Adult Ministry Publishing
LifeWay Church Resources
One LifeWay Plaza
Nashville, Tennessee 37234-0152

We believe the Bible has God for its author; salvation for its end; and truth, without any mixture of error, for its matter and that all Scripture is totally true and trustworthy. To review LifeWay's doctrinal guideline, please visit *www.lifeway.com/doctrinalguideline.com.*

Unless otherwise noted, all Scripture quotations are taken from the Holman Christian Standard Bible®, copyright © 1999, 2000, 2002, 2003, 2009 by Holman Bible Publishers. Used by permission. Holman Christian Standard Bible®, Holman CSB®, and HCSB®are trademarks of Holman Bible Publishers.

Cover design by The Visual Republic

TABLE OF CONTENTS

ICON LEGEND

 Things to
listen to

 Things
to watch

 Expanding on
biblical concepts

 Fun facts and useful
tidbits of information

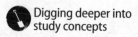 Digging deeper into
study concepts

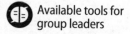 Available tools for
group leaders

On the
Web

ABOUT THE AUTHOR
CHUCK LAWLESS

My name is Chuck, and I'm from Ohio, where I served as a pastor for 14 years before joining the faculty of The Southern Baptist Theological Seminary in Louisville, Kentucky. I was on staff at Southern for 15 years, first as a professor and then as dean of the Billy Graham School of Missions and Evangelism. I now work for the International Mission Board as vice president for Global Theological Advance. Part of my role involves connecting with college and seminary students in North America and around the world.

My wife, Pam, and I were fixed up by two church secretaries, and we've been married now for more than 20 years. We live in the Richmond, Virginia, area. Visit us online at *chucklawless.com*.

Over the years, I've had the privilege of mentoring men who now serve God all around the world. You'll read about some of those experiences in this book. I'm thrilled you want to learn more about mentoring. Thanks for taking the time to read this study—as you do, I pray God would direct you to develop your own mentoring relationships.

WELCOME TO THE MENTOR PROCESS

I love ministering in dirty, crowded, chaotic, never-stopping cities. More than once, I've walked through a city only to find my legs covered in dirt up to my knees when the day ended. Sometimes getting completely clean in these settings means taking several showers, but I'd gladly do it again because of the people I've met, the truths I've learned, and the opportunities I've had. I'm a healthier Christian—more knowledgeable, global, and well-rounded—because of these messy places.

Dirty, dusty places remind me of what it must have been like for Jesus to walk from town to town with His disciples. He spent hour after hour journeying with these men, kicking up the dust, talking about the truth, and investing His life in them. It was a messy process—in terms of the people and the places.

Jesus mentored the men who followed Him. We don't always talk about it in those terms, but it's true. He taught them how to carry on His work. He journeyed through life with them and taught as He went, both by what He said to them and what He did with them. *Mentor* is about this very process Jesus showed us. It's about hanging out with somebody whose life shows

God's power; it's about following Jesus' example and mentoring others so they can carry on Jesus' work too. It's about mentoring and being mentored, discipling and being discipled.

Welcome to this journey. We'll explore how to share our faith by purposefully walking through life together. The sessions in this study are based on Scripture, which I believe is God-inspired (2 Timothy 3:16). They're also written with a certain audience in mind—Christians who desire to be in mentoring relationships with other Christians in the context of a local church or ministry.

Not only will we examine Jesus' practices in mentoring, we'll also look at Paul's work of mentoring in the early church. In the New Testament, Paul and Timothy are classic examples of a mentor and a mentee. Paul, an apostle, church leader, and missionary, mentored Timothy, a young minister and evangelist, who in turn then mentored others in the faith. All of us need to be both a Paul (a mentor) and a Timothy (a mentee). We need to be influenced and to influence others. I hope this study will help you become both.

The road map for our walk together looks like this:

Session one describes the journey of a mentor: Why does that role exist, and what does it look like?

Sessions two and three focus on Jesus and Paul as examples of first-century mentors.

Sessions four and five offer practical tools and strategies for mentoring and being mentored.

And **session six** points out potholes and possibilities we could face as we journey through life together in faith. Sometimes mentoring's messy, but the walk is worth the effort.

> Sometimes mentoring's messy, but the walk is worth the effort.

1

SESSION ONE

UNDERSTANDING
ALONG-THE-WAY DISCIPLESHIP

Think about people who have invited you to walk through a season of life with them. They invested themselves in your life. They gave up their time and gave of themselves. They each helped you in many ways—maybe somebody taught you how to share your testimony, fix a car, be a better spouse, or be a better business person. Somebody else may have shared life with you, modeling Christian living along the way. While not all invested the same level of time and energy, they all made a difference in your world, and that's why you remember them.

My list of these kinds of people is a long one: Randy Richards, Glenn Davidson, Steve Bauer, "Brother Jack" Tichenor, Don Betts, Lawrence Langford, Sonney Allen, Ed Hensley, "Big Dave" Ensor, Ronnie Allen, Ralph Harvey. Their roles have differed—pastors, deacons, laypersons, professors, my fathers in the faith, my father-in-law—but these men and others changed my life. Some earned college and seminary degrees, but not all. Some taught me in Sunday School, and others taught me how to do Sunday School. Some would be surprised that they're even on my list, and that's one of the things I love most about them.

These men have been mentors to me—disciplers, coaches, friends. I've had the privilege of sharing life with some great men of God. Maybe you've had the same privilege. If not, perhaps doing this study will be the catalyst to help you find a mentor or become one.

Who has invested in and influenced your life?

Scott Owens
Melissa Schmidt

How would you describe their motivation for investing in you?

Similar interests in a work-related situation

WHAT'S MENTORING ANYWAY? A SIMPLE DEFINITION
Here's my favorite definition of mentoring: "a God-given relationship in which one growing Christian encourages and equips another believer to reach his/her potential as a disciple of Christ."[1] We'll unpack this definition as we move through this session.

Mentoring is about relationships.

The Bible is filled with stories of discipling relationships. Moses and Aaron. Moses and Joshua. Eli and Samuel. Naomi and Ruth. Elijah and Elisha. Jesus and the disciples. Paul and Timothy. Paul and Titus. Barnabas and John Mark. That's not surprising, since our God is a God of relationships. This is obvious not only by His very nature as Father, Son, and Holy Spirit (2 Corinthians 13:13) but also in the creation story. He created human beings to be in relationship with Himself and each other (Genesis 2:8-25). When He chose to provide salvation, He did it personally by coming to earth, dying as the sacrifice in

Don't miss the short introductory video "Chuck Lawless on Mentoring," available for purchase at *threadsmedia.com*.

our place, and breaking the power of death (Romans 5:12), casting a shadow that would change us forever.

Now, God has given us the church—that is, Christian people—to relate to us, teach us, and guide us. The church loves one another, serves one another, prays for one another, confronts one another, and forgives one another. This body of Christ, when obedient to its marching orders, produces disciples by preaching the gospel and teaching believers (Matthew 28:18-20).

Mentoring builds on divine intersections.

I am amazed at how God orchestrates "divine intersections," those crossroads in which we meet the people He has waiting to mentor us. Brother Jack Tichenor was one divine intersection for me. In many ways, Brother Jack was the mentor who guided me in most of the major decisions I made as a young pastor, though he never officially served as my pastor. I met him after he retired, but he quickly made time for another "preacher boy." Many days I sat with him in his den (or in his garage watching his electric trains go by), and we talked about ministry. He was such a natural mentor that more than 40 young men under his teaching entered the ministry during his 60 years of preaching.

Two things about Brother Jack stuck out to me the most: He never said a negative word about anyone, and he always talked about Jesus. I listened to him share the story of Christ with a stranger in an elevator, a waitress at a restaurant, a patient in a hospital, a visitor at a church service. He was a kind, gentle, older man—so he got away with confrontational evangelism in ways that others might not—and he never missed an opportunity to speak about his Savior. Always focused on Jesus, he saw past the faults of others to see their need for Christ.

I learned more from Brother Jack by watching him relate to others than I did by listening to him talk to me. Our relationship was not a formal mentoring relationship; we had no scheduled meetings or set agendas. Brother Jack probably didn't even think about the fact that I was watching and learning. But I thank God for the divine intersection that allowed our paths to cross.

What divine intersections have you experienced?

I met a woman named Melissa Schmidt when I was organizing and planning VBS. She was such a blessing to talk to and even watch how she lives her life. Fully devoted to Christ.

Listen to "Way of Life" by Echoing Angels from the *Mentor* playlist, available for purchase at *threadsmedia.com*.

Describe the person who is your Brother Jack.

She is 32 years old, married, and has a 3 year old girl. She pursued a career as a social worker but soon became a stay at home mom.

Mentoring requires a growing Christian.

In a mentoring relationship, one person leads and another follows. Somebody must be in front, even if just slightly. Only when we're growing can we guide others toward growth.

Paul was a leading apostle in the early New Testament church and the writer of multiple New Testament letters. He served as a mentor to Timothy, one of the younger early church leaders. Paul could teach Timothy because he kept growing in his own relationship with Jesus (Philippians 3:12-14). When we have a "Paul," whose own growing faith is our example, we can then train our own "Timothy." Our Paul challenges us to grow, and in turn we urge our Timothy to grow also. In this way, mentoring becomes a generational effort as the person I mentor gleans from not only my influence but also the influence of my mentor (and my mentor's mentor and so on).

Thom Rainer probably wouldn't consider himself a Paul to me, but he has been. Thom was my doctoral supervisor and later my boss. What I've learned from him, however, is broader than degrees, job proficiency, or skills related to evangelism and church growth. Over the years, I've watched Thom love his wife and boys through major job changes, a bout with cancer, and the death of a grandson. I've gotten to pinch hit for him when he's canceled commitments because his family needed him. I've seen his boys grow to become best friends with their dad. Even now, despite geographical miles between us, I follow Thom's tweets about his time set aside for his family.

Because I wasn't raised in a Christian home, I need a role model like Thom to help me know how to love my wife. I know the Bible tells me to love Pam as Christ loved the church (Ephesians 5:25), but that doesn't mean I always fully understand how to do that. Men like Thom challenge me to improve as a husband. Then, as I am growing, I can turn around and teach these things to the Timothies in my life.

A mentor has to keep growing spiritually, but mentors are seldom ahead of their disciples in every area of life. Everybody has strengths and weaknesses, and everybody has room for growth. Your mentor (or you as a mentor) might be strong in Bible study but weak in prayer. You may have more passion for personal evangelism than for social justice. A mentor who is single will not be as prepared to give marriage advice as one who is married.

 In Greek mythology, the story of "Mentor" is found in Homer's famous work, *The Odyssey*. When Odysseus, king of Ithaca, went to war, he entrusted the care of his son Telemachus to a friend, Mentor. The term has come to mean someone who is a wise teacher-guide-counselor for another.

As mentors, our goal is to teach out of our strengths and keep working on our weaknesses, so we can continue to grow. That's another reason we need mentors. They point out our weaknesses, challenge us to admit our struggles, give us direction in dealing with those issues, rejoice with us when we experience victory, and love us anyway when we fail. Everybody benefits when our ever-growing mentors keep us moving forward.

Mentoring is a balance of encouraging and equipping.

Following Christ is difficult. A very real enemy fights against us (Ephesians 6:11-12). Trials happen. Disappointments come. Friends sometimes reject our message or betray us. Trusting God is difficult when life seems unfair or the future is unclear. Without encouragement, giving up is a real temptation. This is where mentors can help. Good mentors encourage us when we're stressed and equip us when we need it.

My friend and boss Tom Elliff is a master at encouragement. I've watched him reach out to young pastors and missionaries, reminding them that God is bigger than anything they face and strengthening their faith with his calm presence. When he says, "I'll pray for you," you know he means it. If you have somebody like Tom on your side, you'll press forward through the tough times. That kind of encouragement can make a big difference.

Who encourages you like that? A parent? A teacher? Another believer?

My sister and parents

We need more than encouragement though. In the midst of life's struggles, we also need help doing what God calls us to do. We know we need to study the Bible, but we don't always know where to begin. Pastors tell us prayer matters, but we don't always understand how to pray. Telling others about Jesus is essential, but not always modeled. We don't need someone to tell us what to do as much as how to do it. We need equipping.

Beyond encouraging, mentoring is about teaching Christian disciplines and life skills. Encouragement without equipping might lead to restored hope, but seldom does it produce life transformation—the goal of mentoring.

When I first started mentoring many years ago, I assumed I would be focusing almost exclusively on teaching spiritual disciplines like Bible study, prayer, and fasting. Since then, I've met young people who are looking to be equipped in many more areas. The list is extensive: understanding the opposite gender, relating to parents, budgeting, retirement planning, buying life insurance, understanding God's will, playing racquetball, grilling a steak, buying a house, writing a resumé, finding a church, dealing with a health crisis, overcoming temptation, raising kids, purchasing a car, painting a wall, and on and on. That's life-on-life equipping.

From your experience, have your fellow believers been better at encouraging you or equipping you? Explain.

Encouraging. I have found that most people would rather encourage than equip because its less time-consuming and seems easier.

Describe one area where you need equipping.

In my personal quiet time in the ~~used~~ word / prayer time

Mentoring is about transformation.

The goal of Christian mentoring is that the disciple becomes more like Jesus and then leads others to do the same. It's hard to find a loftier goal. Mentoring matters in an eternal way. In the next section (and in session three of this study), we'll focus on some of the apostle Paul's writing to Titus, one of Paul's disciples among the early church leaders (2 Corinthians 8:16-17,23). Titus was to challenge people to invest their lives in other believers, just as Paul had invested his life in Titus's. Paul expected believers to fulfill this calling, because he knew what God was doing behind the scenes:

> **"For those He foreknew He also predestined to be conformed to the image of His Son, so that He would be the firstborn among many brothers" (Romans 8:29).**

Titus is one of three New Testament books (along with 1 and 2 Timothy) commonly known as the "Pastoral Letters." These letters include instructions from Paul to his own protégés in the faith as they worked to address specific issues in New Testament churches.

According to this verse, if you're a follower of Jesus, God is in the process of making you more like His Son. The word *conformed* speaks of God's changing us, remaking us so our lives model Christ's. Ultimately, God will change us completely in heaven, so we'll be like His Son. But while we're here on earth, He moves us in that direction. We call this process *sanctification*, defined by one theologian as "a progressive work of God and man that makes us more and more free from sin and like Christ in our actual lives."[2] Letting go of sin and becoming more like Jesus are two elements of this transformation.

God alone gives us victory as He makes us like Christ, that's for sure. But we cooperate with Him in this process. We're expected to do the legwork of turning away from sin and daily putting our faith in God as our source of all things. These verses reveal the choices we need to make to do our part as God transforms us:

> **"But now you must also put away all the following: anger, wrath, malice, slander, and filthy language from your mouth. Do not lie to one another, since you have put off the old self with its practices and have put on the new self. You are being renewed in knowledge according to the image of your Creator" (Colossians 3:8-10).**

> **"Therefore, since we also have such a large cloud of witnesses surrounding us, let us lay aside every weight and the sin that so easily ensnares us. Let us run with endurance the race that lies before us, keeping our eyes on Jesus, the source and perfecter of our faith, who for the joy that lay before Him endured a cross and despised the shame and has sat down at the right hand of God's throne" (Hebrews 12:1-2).**

> **"Therefore, ridding yourselves of all moral filth and evil, humbly receive the implanted word, which is able to save you. But be doers of the word and not hearers only, deceiving yourselves" (James 1:21-22).**

> **"Therefore, with your minds ready for action, be serious and set your hope completely on the grace to be brought to you at the revelation of Jesus Christ" (1 Peter 1:13).**

How does our active role in sanctification fit into the concept of mentoring? It applies to both the mentors, who are responsible for their own spiritual legwork, and the people being mentored, who need to be encouraged in their spiritual legwork. Titus had the responsibility of walking in faith as these Scriptures describe, but he also had Paul as a mentor to help him figure out how to do that. Their mentoring relationship probably encouraged both of them in this effort.

Paul urged his disciples to follow his example and thereby follow Jesus (see 1 Corinthians 11:1). He expected the people he mentored to mature in Christ, and he modeled Christianity in front of them and alongside them as they aimed for spiritual growth. Those who were mentored by Paul were becoming more and more like Jesus in the process. This is the key to mentoring.

Think back to the Great Commission: We're to "make disciples." To be like Jesus is to be willing to reproduce ourselves in disciples, release them to do ministry, and support them as they invest in others—just as Jesus did. This is a foundational truth: Mentors who invest in others as Jesus did will produce other mentors and lives will be transformed.

Who do you know who is growing to be more and more like Jesus?

Ashley & Pike

Who is more like Jesus because of spending time with you?

Shelby Edblad

WHAT ABOUT MENTORING IN THE EARLY CHURCH? A BIBLICAL DESCRIPTION
Several years ago, a student asked me if I'd be his mentor. My approach has always been to ask for a description of what a potential mentee wants, and I did the same with this student. Here's what he wrote for me in an e-mail: "I don't really want accountability, and I'm not that much interested in talking about spiritual disciplines. I'd just like to hang out." There's a place for "just hanging out" in mentoring, but biblical mentoring is more intentional and directed than what this student wanted. Compare my student's thinking to the directions for mentoring that Paul sent to Titus.

> **"But you must say the things that are consistent with sound teaching. Older men are to be level headed, worthy of respect, sensible, and sound in faith, love, and endurance. In the same way, older women are to be reverent in behavior, not slanderers, not addicted to much wine. They are to teach what is good, so they may encourage the young women to**

 "Paul wrote multiple times commanding converts to, 'Be ye followers of me.' Their Bible first had legs." –Waylon Moore, mentoring expert (*mentoring-disciples.org*)

love their husbands and to love their children, to be self-controlled, pure, homemakers, kind, and submissive to their husbands, so that God's message will not be slandered. In the same way, encourage the young men to be self-controlled in everything. Make yourself an example of good works with integrity and dignity in your teaching. Your message is to be sound beyond reproach, so that the opponent will be ashamed, having nothing bad to say about us" (Titus 2:1-8).

Mentoring crosses generations.

Titus was working with the Christians in Crete, a poorly organized congregation threatened by false teachers. One solution to the problems in Crete was for growing believers to ground younger believers in the Christian faith. Older men (most likely men who were old enough to have raised families of their own) were to model Christian living by being clearheaded, respectable, and sensible. Their lives were to be characterized by good judgment and Christian dignity, their faith grounded in true doctrine, their love for God and others genuine, and their patience under trial obvious. This passage suggests that the older men were to model their faith particularly for the younger men in the church.

Sonney Allen modeled his faith in this way for me. Sonney was a deacon in the first church where I served as pastor. I was young (early 20s), and Sonney was a more mature believer. He hadn't attended college or seminary, but he was fully educated in life. He taught me about remodeling a home, doing evangelism, and loving all kinds of people. I watched him as he loved his wife and son with a deep, sacrificial love. Similarly, I knew he loved me regardless of whether I made bad or good decisions. As a young pastor, I needed that kind of support.

Sonney later developed multiple illnesses. His pain was great, yet I never heard him complain. He still laughed, worshiped, and shared the gospel even as he was dying. Just before he died, I was honored to dedicate my doctoral dissertation to him. That was the least I could do for a mentor who showed me how to live as a godly man should.

The passage in Titus also has direction for older women to mentor younger women. These older women (old enough to have raised their families) were to live lives of reverence, not gossiping or overindulging in wine. They were to teach "what is good," not by formal schooling but by informal life-on-life modeling. Specifically, it was their responsibility to train younger women how to live out their Christian faith. They were to teach them to love their husbands and children, to be self-controlled and pure, to take care of their homes in kindness, and to graciously follow their husband's direction. By living holy lives and teaching others to do the same, the older women would honor God's Word.

 The term "homemakers" in Titus 2:5 doesn't mean that a woman can't work outside of the home, but that the home should be the central place of ministry for a wife and mother.

It might surprise us to read that the older women were instructed to teach younger women such basic Christian responsibilities. Keep in mind, though, that this was still a new faith with a lifestyle ethic that was counterpoint to the worldview of the day. Even loving children as gifts from God rather than merely as economic blessings (particularly sons) was a radically different mind-set. Younger women needed older Christian women to show them the way.

Mary, a member of a church where I served, modeled this kind of cross-generational mentoring among women. She taught a young ladies' Bible study class, but her primary influence came more informally as she opened her home to these ladies. Most often seated at the table with a cup of coffee in hand, Mary patiently and lovingly gave advice when asked. Some of the women studied the Bible with her, and they later became teachers themselves. In at least one situation, Mary helped someone find employment. Today, many women would proudly point out that Mary met the requirements of Titus 2 in their lives.

For the men: What older man has been most influential in your life? How would you describe his investment?

For the women: What older woman has been most influential in your life? What words would you use to describe her?

Mentoring is done by those who are spiritually mature.

After addressing older men and women, Paul turned his attention to Titus. Even as a younger man, Titus was to model Christian faithfulness for other young men. Whatever his age, a man growing in his faith, like Titus, has something to invest in other young men.

Listen to "Jesus Use Me I'm Yours (Derek Webb Remix)" by Jason Gray from the *Mentor* playlist, available for purchase at *threadsmedia.com*.

Titus could model basic holy living by doing good deeds, discerning right doctrine, and exhibiting dignity and seriousness. Titus's words, whether as formal teaching or informal conversation, were to be so biblically consistent that even his opponents would have no case against him.

Here we learn a simple truth about mentoring: While mentoring downward through spiritual generations—older to younger—is essential, it's not the only model for mentoring. You don't always have to be older than people to be their mentor. Investing in others requires only that you're one step ahead in some area—that you've learned something you can turn around and give to others. Whatever your age, life experience and Christian growth make the most effective tools for mentors.

Mentoring requires self-control.

Notice how many times in this passage Paul called believers to be self-controlled. The older men and women and the younger men and women were asked to show self-restraint and mature judgment. They were to maintain control of their passions, thoughts, and words. Apparently this was a significant issue for the believers in Crete, perhaps because some of the heresy that was running through the group was the idea that Christians could live however they wanted without regard for morality.

Exhibiting self-control in an out-of-control culture isn't easy. One way to learn that kind of maturity is by watching others and allowing them to train you, that is, through mentoring. It's one thing to listen to people tell us to be self-controlled; it's another matter to stand in the shadows and watch them maintain control when they're wrongly accused, treated unfairly, dealing with a disappointment, or stubbing their toes. A Titus 2 ministry looks like this: Believers who have "been there" train others who haven't, so when they get there, they'll honor God with how they live. The evidence of our faith is best seen in day-to-day living.

Review the varied characteristics that Paul told Titus the believers must attain (self-control, a level-head, worthy of respect, sensible, sound in faith, etc.). In your opinion, which are most difficult to achieve and why?

 For a glimpse into a mentoring relationship in action, watch the video "Jason and Jordan's Story," available for purchase at *threadsmedia.com*.

Why do you think Paul emphasized self-control within each age and gender group?

WHY DOES IT MATTER? REASONS FOR MENTORING

Most church discipleship ministries are organized programmatically. That is, they center around small groups and directed Bible studies. Their success is often based on numbers attending. But this model misses the most obvious New Testament means of disciple-making: one-on-one, face-to-face mentoring. We should still invest our time and ourselves in this basic, relational model for many reasons.[3]

Mentoring is biblical.

Jesus produced disciples by investing first in a group of 12 men and then, more pointedly, in three of those men. He called them to be with Him, taught them, empowered them, prayed before them, sent them out, challenged them, called them to account, and even fixed a meal for them. They in turn became leaders in the early church.

The apostle Paul followed Jesus' model by pouring his life into a few young men such as Timothy. This young protégé watched Paul minister, walked in his shadow, rejoiced with him when lives were changed, and prayed for him when he was persecuted. What joy Paul must have felt knowing that after he was gone, Timothy would carry on the work of spreading the gospel.

If Jesus and Paul made disciples through this means, it's a good pattern for us to follow.

Mentoring reinforces the truth of the Word.

When we watch our mentors share their faith, we're more likely to share our own faith. Spouses with godly marriages give us the invaluable gift of seeing Christian homes in motion. Life becomes an effective classroom. We get to see in action what we hear in the Word. So many of God's truths have come to life for me within the context of watching somebody else.

As a young man, John went through a difficult divorce after an even more difficult marriage. When he heard the gospel and received God's forgiveness after his divorce, he experienced forgiveness in a profound way. Grace meant so much to him that he lived his life reaching out to others who the church often rejected. In the few years that our lives intersected as leaders in the same congregation, I viewed God's mercy differently because I saw it lived out in John's life.

Jim grew up in a Christian home, and his parents were his primary mentors. I met Jim when the church where he was a deacon called me as their pastor. I was young, untrained, and struggling to trust all of God's promises. Jim, on the other hand, had seen God keep His Word so many times over the years that it made no sense not to trust Him. He read Jesus' words, "So don't worry, saying, 'What will we eat?' or 'What will we drink?' or 'What will we wear?'" (Matthew 6:31), and Jim accepted them without doubt. I never knew him to worry. It was my privilege to be influenced by this man.

Mentoring requires the mentor to guard his or her life against the Enemy's attacks.

If you choose to be a Christian mentor, you'll wear a bull's eye on your back for Satan. If he can seriously wound the mentor, those who follow will bear the scars of that fall. Never does a mentor fall without a ripple effect. Understanding that, if you choose to be a mentor, you must guard yourself.

Why do we hear so often about people in leadership, who have great influence over the people watching them, falling to the Enemy's attacks? J. D. Greear, a pastor in North Carolina, argues that our living in isolation contributes to the moral failures plaguing our culture. God created us to be in relationship with Him and others, and anything less than that opens the door for Satan. Dr. Greear says, "God never intended any of us to live alone. Deep friendships with people you live and work and go to church with is a part of discipleship. The shepherd is still a sheep."[4] The shepherd fights the same battles that the other sheep fight.

This confirms our earlier definition of mentoring: "a God-given relationship in which one growing Christian encourages and equips another believer to reach his/her potential as a disciple of Christ." Mentoring creates a positive cycle of sorts. Good mentors stand their ground against the Enemy because they don't want to harm their witness before their mentees. And in the very practice of mentoring, they're keeping themselves in relationship with other growing Christians, which thus reinforces their ability to stand that ground.

Who's watching your life? Who would know if you fell?

 We don't hear the word *mentee* often. Although it sounds like a marine animal, it's the term for a person in the process of being mentored or discipled. Some people use *mentoree*.

What steps do you consider essential to guard your life against the Enemy's attacks?

Mentoring relationships offer a safe place to deal with failure.

Outside of mentoring relationships, believers have no one to hold them accountable in their faith walks. Mentors model holiness, call their disciples to the same, and hold them accountable to that standard.

What about when disciples fail to meet that standard? In that case, the mentor has the opportunity to model the kind of forgiveness, grace, and mercy that enables the people being mentored to correct their course and return to the fight. In mentoring relationships, confession is essential—people need to be utterly honest. Spiritual full disclosure brings our sin out of the Enemy's darkness into God's light where we can deal with it through repentance and forgiveness.

Mentors who grant grace to people who have failed aren't ignoring or negating the consequences of sin. Instead, they're modeling God's love to fallen but repentant people. Good mentoring creates an atmosphere for honest confession because the mentee knows that admitting the truth will not result in any less love or acceptance.

In this kind of relationship, spiritual growth occurs in two directions: the mentor strives for holiness out of obedience to God and love for the mentee, and the mentee chooses obedience out of gratitude to God for His mercy shown through the mentor. In effective mentoring, safety in failure leads to less failure.

Mentoring produces the next generation of Christian leaders.

I keep in my files a Father's Day card from a student in whom I invested significant time. The message on the card is simple, but it speaks like a megaphone to me: "Thanks for being a father in my life." That card encourages me to press on when I get tired of the bureaucracy, paperwork, meetings, and tedious tasks that sometimes accompany an administrative job. This kind of divine intersection is one of the greatest benefits of mentoring.

Mentoring is costly. We have to prioritize; spending time with others usually means deleting something else from the calendar. We have to put our egos aside; our own sins

 Confession means "to say the same thing about, to agree with." When we confess, we agree with God about our sin.

are magnified when others are watching. We often have to spend money; the costs of study resources, shared meals, and occasional travel expenses quickly add up. We may be misunderstood; mentors sometimes get accused of having favorites. And too often we experience disappointment; mentees often fail. Any mentor might wonder at times if mentoring is worth the effort.

Being mentored is also risky. Your mentor might disappoint you. You might expect more than he or she can give. The push to live a holy life and maintain accountability might make you uncomfortable. You may not want to invest in somebody else in turn.

On the other hand, the risks you take as you're mentored might result in the amazing gift of an invaluable friendship. God might give you a mentor and friend whose faith challenges you to greater faithfulness. The risks you take as you mentor others may result in disciples whose faith is potent and whose progress is obvious. You may grow spiritually like never before, and you might watch God use the people you've discipled in ways you'd never dreamed. You might get a father, son, mother, or daughter in the faith.

I'll take that risk any day.

THROUGH THE WEEK

> **CONNECT:** Make a list of the people who have been "Pauls" for you. Make a phone call, send an e-mail, or write a letter—say thanks. Let them know what you've gained by walking through life with them.

> **PRAY:** If you don't currently have a mentor, begin asking God to provide one.

> **OBSERVE:** Watch for divine intersections in your life this week.

 Leading a group? It's the way to go. Find session videos, extra questions, and teaching tools in the *Mentor* leader kit, available for purchase in print or downloadable form at *threadsmedia.com*.

2

SESSION TWO

LEARNING FROM THE MASTER: JESUS & HIS DISCIPLES

Remember the WWJD bracelets people wore as a reminder to ask, "What Would Jesus Do?" This movement was popularized in the 1990s in the United States, and the number of people who wore the bracelet has been estimated anywhere from 15 million to as high as 52 million.

We don't have to wonder what Jesus would do because we know what He did. He made disciples. He mentored His followers in the faith. So when it comes to mentoring, it's not "What *Would* Jesus Do?"; it's "What *Did* Jesus Do?"

MAKING DISCIPLES: JESUS' COMMAND

Not long before the resurrected Jesus returned to His Father, He met His followers on a mountainside in Galilee. There, He gave them these marching orders:

> **"Then Jesus came near and said to them, 'All authority has been given to Me in heaven and on earth. Go, therefore, and make disciples of all nations, baptizing them in the name of the Father and of the Son and of the Holy Spirit, teaching them to observe everything I have commanded you. And remember, I am with you always, to the end of the age'" (Matthew 28:18-20).**

The Great Commission is familiar to anyone who has spent much time in an evangelical church. Sometimes we hear the word "go" as the command in this text, but the clearest command in the original Greek language is "make disciples." Making disciples isn't optional for followers of Jesus.

If making disciples is imperative, we must understand what the phrase actually means. It's a two-sided coin. On one side is an invitation to enter into a relationship with the Master, Jesus, and follow His teachings. This step is what we sometimes call "conversion," when we turn from our sin and trust Christ for salvation. That conversion is publicly illustrated by the act of baptism.

On the other side of the coin is a call to Christian growth through obeying (or "observing") everything Jesus commanded us to do. We often call this process "discipleship." Those who choose to walk in Jesus' path will know and follow His teachings—including His order to teach others His commands. Therefore, making disciples should result in more disciples who make even more disciples.

Here's how one scholar describes this two-sided coin of discipleship: "If those outside of the faith aren't hearing the gospel and being challenged to make a decision for Christ, then the church has disobeyed one part of Jesus' commission. If new converts aren't faithfully and lovingly nurtured in the whole counsel of God's revelation, then the church has disobeyed the other part."[1]

It's the "other part" that's the focus here. If we must follow Jesus' teachings, how do new believers know those teachings? How will they learn about Christian standards for relationships, morality, or giving? How will they know what Jesus expects? There's only one answer: Someone must teach them. We can't expect untaught believers to obey commands they don't know. Mentors who make disciples are necessary in the church, and equally important are believers who desire to be mentored in their walk with Jesus.

....

 Charles Sheldon was the author of *In His Steps*, the fictional story of a church challenged to ask, "What would Jesus do?" before doing anything. Published in 1896, its question still dominates Christian thought.

Think about the churches you've attended. Were most better at evangelizing or discipling?

Why do you think Jesus started the Great Commission with "all authority has been given to Me"?

Making disciples through mentoring is personal.

Four additional expressions of the Great Commission can be found in the New Testament:

> "Then He said to them, 'Go into all the world and preach the gospel to the whole creation'" (Mark 16:15).

> "Then He opened their minds to understand the Scriptures. He also said to them, 'This is what is written: The Messiah would suffer and rise from the dead the third day, and repentance for forgiveness of sins would be proclaimed in His name to all the nations, beginning at Jerusalem. You are witnesses of these things'" (Luke 24:45-48).

> "Jesus said to them again, 'Peace to you! As the Father has sent Me, I also send you'" (John 20:21).

> "[Y]ou will be My witnesses in Jerusalem, in all Judea and Samaria, and to the ends of the earth" (Acts 1:8).

Some writers believe that more than Jesus' 11 remaining disciples heard Him speak the Great Commission. That's possible, but the number of hearers isn't the point. The point is that Jesus' words are meant personally for every believer. As the Father sent Him, Jesus in His authority sends His followers to proclaim the Word and make disciples. Each of us must do evangelism and mentor those who come to faith.

What are you doing to fulfill the Great Commission? If you aren't doing anything, have a conversation with someone who can help you figure out how to start.

 The word translated as *disciple* means "a learner, one who follows a teaching." This term occurs approximately 250 times in the New Testament as either "disciple" or "disciples."

Making disciples through mentoring is global.

While the word "go" isn't a command in the original Greek text of Matthew 28:19 in the same way that it's translated in English, that's not to say the Great Commission doesn't require us to make disciples of people around the world. In fact, four of the five Great Commission passages in the New Testament clearly speak of the nations or the world. It's our responsibility to make disciples of all "nations," a word that most likely refers to ethnic people groups rather than geopolitical countries.

What does this command mean to you? It might mean that God has a mentor/mentee for you from a different ethnic group. You may find believers from other countries who have had significant gospel training. On occasion, someone from a different cultural perspective can challenge our faith to a level of discomfort—and growth.

Years ago, I met several international students and church leaders at a conference I was leading in East Asia. My topic was prayer, and my responsibility was to teach these students about praying effectively. I taught for several hours then prayed aloud for a few minutes, inviting the students to pray along with me. For the next hour, these students gave me a lesson in prayer. Their prayers were gut-level, gripping cries to the Lord. They spoke to God not with the vocabulary of a seminary professor, but with the authentic pangs of people who wanted God to do something mighty. My official role that day was teacher, yet I was the one taught. These believers weren't officially my mentors; nevertheless, I was honored to sit at their feet and learn more about prayer and trust and passion.

The global nature of the Great Commission calls us to consider serving as mentors to internationals in our communities who follow Jesus. God may bring a foreign exchange student, immigrant, or even a refugee believer to your area in order to form a divine intersection with you. Don't miss that opportunity to be obedient to Jesus' Great Commission command.

How many international citizens do you cross paths with during your week?

What challenges could arise in mentoring someone from a different culture?

MAKING DISCIPLES: JESUS' METHOD

Jesus told His disciples to make disciples, and He modeled for them how to do that. Let's look at how Jesus mentored and learn from His approach.

Jesus called His disciples in the context of relationships.

Jesus' approach to mentoring was a process, especially as He called His twelve disciples. Contrary to what we sometimes think, Jesus called these men in stages. As you read about these stages, think about people in your life who are in various stages of a relationship with you. Some may be just acquaintances. Others may be long-term friends. All who are Christians are candidates for a mentor or mentee.

Stage One: The Call to Follow

The Gospel of John tells us that Jesus met some of His future disciples when John the Baptist first pointed them to Him:

> **"Again the next day, John was standing with two of his disciples. When he saw Jesus passing by, he said, 'Look! The Lamb of God!' The two disciples heard him say this and followed Jesus. When Jesus turned and noticed them following Him, He asked them, 'What are you looking for?' They said to Him, 'Rabbi' (which means 'Teacher'), 'where are You staying?' 'Come and you'll see,' He replied. So they went and saw where He was staying, and they stayed with Him that day. It was about 10 in the morning"** (John 1:35-39).

John the Baptist, the forerunner of Jesus, knew that his calling was to point others to Jesus. Two of his disciples, Andrew and likely John the son of Zebedee, followed his direction by pursuing Jesus. John's enthusiasm toward Christ was so great that John's disciples left him behind and followed after Christ, seeking a personal conversation with Him. Jesus saw them following Him and spent the day with them.

You, too, can be sensitive to what's happening spiritually in the lives of people around you. You can learn from somebody who's growing so obviously in his or her walk with Jesus. There's potentially someone else who's battling in his or her Christianity, and you could help. Maybe there's a new believer, excited but confused about the next steps to

 Listen to "Faithful Still" by Tara Leigh Cobble from the *Mentor* playlist, available for purchase at *threadsmedia.com*.

take in his or her faith. Raise your spiritual antenna and watch for opportunities in the relationships God gives you.

Whose spiritual life is so attractive to you that you would want that person to be your mentor?

Is your spiritual life so strong that others would want you to be their mentor? Who do you think is most closely following your lead?

Stage Two: The Call to Full-time Service

The story with John the Baptist is the first recorded encounter between Jesus and five of His potential disciples. He was their teacher, and they trusted Him. But they hadn't yet walked away from their regular jobs. That step didn't happen until Jesus called them to leave everything behind to become "fishers of men" (Luke 5:1-11). In response to that call, they dropped it all and followed Him.

In mentoring, it's not our responsibility to call people to give up their jobs; God doesn't call everyone to full-time ministry. He does, however, demand first place in our lives. The First Commandment makes that clear—anything that keeps us from serving God wholeheartedly is an idol that must be forsaken (Exodus 20:3). In the mentoring process, we're called to make God the priority of our lives.

Stage Three: The Call to Apostle

In the last stage of the disciples' calling, Jesus chose 12 men to be apostles, "ones sent with a message." These were the disciples who Jesus would most closely mentor.

> **"During those days He went out to the mountain to pray and spent all night in prayer to God. When daylight came, He summoned His disciples, and He chose 12 of them—He also named them apostles" (Luke 6:12-13).**

We can learn a lot from Jesus' choosing the Twelve. First, Jesus prayed. All night long, in fact. From His larger group of followers, Jesus then selected His mentees. Second, Jesus initiated the relationship. He didn't wait for mentees to come to Him. He intentionally sought out those who would walk most closely with Him. Third, Jesus selected ordinary men. They weren't religious leaders or trained teachers. Rather, they were uneducated

---

 Researchers tell us there are 16,000-plus people groups around the world. Of these, more than 6,000 are considered "unreached" or "least reached" with the gospel. Check out *joshuaproject.net* for more information.

and unknown. Fourth, Jesus called them to Him for a purpose. He would send them out, and they would carry His message throughout the Roman Empire. Mentoring would result in ministry.

How would you feel if someone asked to be your mentor?

How would you feel if someone asked you to mentor them?

Jesus spent time with His disciples.

The Gospel of Mark is the shortest of the four Gospels. It's action-packed, with fewer extensive teaching segments than the other Gospels. A quick look at Mark's record shows that Jesus shared life with His disciples. They watched Him heal the sick, exorcise demons, confront religious leaders, calm storms, raise the dead, walk on water, multiply food, and overturn tables. These men heard Him answer questions, preach to crowds, silence demons, speak parables, and pray to the Father. They ate with Him, discussed truth with Him, and ministered alongside Him.

All of that was possible because Jesus spent quality time with His disciples. Indeed, He called them first to be with Him (Mark 3:14), and their time with Him changed their world. Mentoring means that we give a mentee much more than a book or a conference; we give ourselves to another person for the sake of the gospel.

When I teach mentoring conferences, I always ask this question: "What do you think keeps people from entering into a mentoring relationship, either as mentor or as one being mentored?" The answers vary. Fear of vulnerability often hinders the potential mentor. An unwillingness to commit to meetings gets in the way of possible mentees. Both groups are often unclear about the details of mentoring, especially if they've never been in mentoring relationships. Overwhelmingly, though, the biggest perceived hindrance to mentoring is a lack of time.

Jesus and His disciples dealt with that objection. He simply made the time to be with them, and they prioritized their commitment to be with Him. That's the way mentoring should work.

 Mark, the Gospel writer, wasn't one of Jesus' disciples. It's likely that Simon Peter was his human source for the stories in his Gospel.

Jesus gave His disciples tasks . . . and held them accountable.

Imagine following Jesus to the top of a mountain where His garments are changed to a brilliant white. Then, think about bowing in amazement when, still at the top of this mountain, Moses and Elijah show up—the lawgiver and the prophet of Old Testament history who have been deceased for centuries.

> **"About eight days after these words, He took along Peter, John, and James and went up on the mountain to pray. As He was praying, the appearance of His face changed, and His clothes became dazzling white. Suddenly, two men were talking with Him—Moses and Elijah. They appeared in glory and were speaking of His death, which He was about to accomplish in Jerusalem. Peter and those with him were in a deep sleep, and when they became fully awake, they saw His glory and the two men who were standing with Him. As the two men were departing from Him, Peter said to Jesus, 'Master, it's good for us to be here! Let us make three tabernacles: one for You, one for Moses, and one for Elijah'—not knowing what he said. While he was saying this, a cloud appeared and overshadowed them. They became afraid as they entered the cloud. Then a voice came from the cloud, saying: This is My Son, the Chosen One; listen to Him!" (Luke 9:28-35).**

Imagine God's voice saying, "This is My Son . . . listen to Him." It's no wonder Peter stated the obvious, "It's good for us to be here!" Who would've known what to say in the midst of such a miracle? How would you respond?

Peter didn't want to leave; instead, he wanted to build a tabernacle to mark this place. But Jesus wouldn't allow His disciples to stay on that mountain. There was still work for Him to do. There was still work for the disciples to do, too—following in obedience, sharing the good news, and making more disciples. More immediately, a young boy possessed with a demon needed Jesus' help. For that reason, Jesus went with His disciples back down the mountain to do His work. Good mentoring should always lead to godly action.

Jesus taught His mentees and expected them to act on His teachings. Luke 9–10 describe this sending out process, including Jesus' instructions (9:1-6; 10:1-11). He sent them out to take on demons. He challenged them to figure out a way to feed more than 5,000 people when they had far too little food. He required them to pray for more laborers, even while they went out to preach and heal in His name.

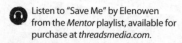

Listen to "Save Me" by Elenowen from the *Mentor* playlist, available for purchase at *threadsmedia.com*.

Upon their return, they gave Jesus a report of their travels. When they rejoiced in their spiritual power rather than in God's grace, He loved them enough to correct them—don't be excited about your power over demons, be excited about your acceptance from God (Luke 10:18-20). These interactions between Jesus and His apostles show us that accountability is a part of Christlike mentoring. Jesus had expectations of those who followed Him. He didn't love them any less when those expectations went unmet, but He always called His followers to grow. We should do the same.

Jesus gave His life for His disciples.

The death of Jesus is central to our Christian faith. Apart from Jesus' shedding His blood for us, we can't be saved (Hebrews 9:22). Jesus' cross shows us just how much He loved His disciples—and how much He loves us. We don't ordinarily give our lives for those we mentor in this same way. But we can love in such a way that we're *willing* to give our lives for them.

Tony Dungy was the coach of the Super Bowl-winning Indianapolis Colts. One of Dungy's heroes was John Thompson Jr., former coach of the Georgetown University Hoyas. When Coach Thompson heard that a notorious drug dealer was influencing his Georgetown players, he confronted the dealer personally and directly. Listen to Dungy's reflections on that risky action:

> "I immediately thought of Jesus' parable of the sheep and the shepherd in the Gospel of John, chapter 10. There, Jesus speaks of the difference between a hired hand and a shepherd. When a wolf comes and threatens the flock, the hired hand runs away, leaving the sheep—someone else's sheep—to fend for themselves. The shepherd, on the other hand, rises to the defense of his sheep. He will *die* for the sheep, if necessary, because they are *his* . . . I had to take a look in the mirror to determine whether I was exhibiting this relational quality: I cared about those I was leading, but was I willing to die for them if that became necessary for their well-being? I hoped the answer was yes, but I wasn't sure that it was—yet."[2]

That's doing for a mentee what Jesus would do—giving up your life. Imagine being one of the players that coach was protecting. It's easier to follow someone's leadership when you know that person is staking his or her life on you.

We don't often get such a dramatic opportunity to show people their value to us, but there are many ways that, in Christ's name, we can give up our lives for those who follow us—the choices we make to be the kinds of people they need to follow, the time we give,

---

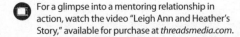

For a glimpse into a mentoring relationship in action, watch the video "Leigh Ann and Heather's Story," available for purchase at *threadsmedia.com*.

the opportunities we turn down. Any of these sacrifices, for the sake of investing ourselves in others in the hopes of helping them become more like Jesus, is a godly sacrifice.

Think of a person you know you're important to. How does the value that person puts on you affect the way you listen to him or her?

Describe a time when someone sacrificed for you.

MAKING DISCIPLES: JESUS' POWER AND PRESENCE
Do you remember how many expressions of the Great Commission there are in the New Testament? The answer is five: Matthew 28, Mark 16, Luke 24, John 20, and Acts 1. Each of these Scripture passages is about the church being sent to all people groups to tell the gospel and make disciples. These passages also include a promise of power within the promise of presence:

> **"And remember, I am with you always, to the end of the age"**
> **(Matthew 28:20).**

> **"And look, I am sending you what My Father promised. As for you, stay in the city until you are empowered from on high" (Luke 24:49).**

> **"After saying this, He breathed on them and said, 'Receive the Holy Spirit'"**
> **(John 20:22).**

> **"But you will receive power when the Holy Spirit has come on you . . . "**
> **(Acts 1:8).**

Jesus, in His authority as the Son of God, ordered us to make disciples—sharing the gospel and teaching believers. Then, He assured us of the power to get the job done. The Father promised to empower us, the Son is ever with us, and the Spirit has come upon us. What else do we need?

The Spirit empowers us to teach the Word of God boldly and powerfully (Acts 4:8,31). He produces the fruit of the Spirit in us (Galatians 5:22-23) and gives us spiritual gifts to use in ministry (1 Corinthians 12:11). When we seek truth, the Spirit guides us there (John 14:17; 15:26). When we don't know how to pray, He intercedes for us (Romans 8:26-27). The Spirit of God lives in us, and He gives us what we need to be growing mentors and mentees. We don't mentor in and of our own strength. We don't have to worry or wonder if we'll know what to say at the right time or how to deal with every situation. We can simply walk through life with those we mentor, knowing that God's presence and power are waiting at every turn.

Jesus' Power in Modern Mentors

I wish you could have met my friend Christie. Though she became a believer in Christ at a young age, it wasn't until her adult years that she began to grow as a disciple. Christie was wise, especially in crisis. Very little threatened her inner calm as she trusted God with a childlike faith. In some ways, she was a "crisis mentor" for many young women who turned to her when perceived emergencies stole their peace. Christie was the mentor, but the Holy Spirit was really her power and peace.

I wish I could introduce you to David. He's one of the guys I mentor, even though we're separated geographically by thousands of miles. (I thank God for the Internet and Skype!) David can be strong-willed at times, but he always comes around to being malleable and teachable. His humility—an indicator that the Spirit of God is working in him—makes him a great friend to mentor. I'm excited about what the Lord plans to do in His power through David as he in turn mentors others.

How do we tap into this power that's promised in Scripture so it's evident in our mentoring relationships? First, we admit we can't do it on our own. None of us can live holy lives in our own strength, and none can change somebody else's life. We all default toward pride, not humility. We're self-absorbed, by nature, and that trait makes us less than ideal mentors and mentees. Let's just admit together that we can't do well in a mentoring relationship apart from God's power.

After admitting we can't do this on our own, we trust God for His power. To know God and recognize His authority are to understand that we live victoriously only through Him. Think about it. God is the warrior who led His people across the Red Sea (Exodus 15:3). David fought the Philistine giant not with a sword and a javelin, but in the name of the

Lord whose battle it was (1 Samuel 17:45-47). Jehaziel likewise assured Jehoshaphat of God's presence in the midst of battle with these words: "This is what the LORD says: 'Do not be afraid or discouraged because of this vast number, for the battle is not yours, but God's'" (2 Chronicles 20:15). We are to put on God's armor, not ours (Ephesians 6:11).

Finally, we pray, following the lead of men and women of faith. Abraham, Moses, Nehemiah, David, Jeremiah, Daniel, and others prayed. Hannah and Mary prayed. Jesus prayed in the morning, into the evening, and through the night. He prayed passionately for His followers and for those who would follow after them. The disciples asked for lessons on prayer. Peter and Paul prayed. When we admit our need for God, then trust His power, then connect with Him through prayer, we tap into the power of God to form strong mentoring relationships.

Jesus' Power at Work

Imagine a blank sheet of paper in front of you. On that paper, list all the reasons you can think of to keep you from mentoring someone else. Your list might look like this: too little time, don't know enough, afraid of vulnerability, don't know where to start, not sure who the mentee would be, never mentored before, and so on.

Then, envision a separate list of reasons for not being mentored. Your list might overlap with the first one, but it will probably include other reasons, too: not sure what being mentored would involve, not enough time, afraid of being vulnerable, don't want to be accountable, not sure anyone would want to invest in me. . . .

Finally, take a separate sheet of paper and write the words, "The Power and Presence of God." In your mind, lay that second sheet across the first one, completely covering your excuses with the power of God. Let the final image sink in for a few minutes.

The picture in your mind should be clear. Jesus commanded us to make disciples, and He empowers us to be obedient to His command. That combination means we have no excuse not to make disciples through mentoring.

What reasons would you give for not being in a mentoring relationship?

What reason to be a mentor is greater than all of the reasons not to?

MAKING DISCIPLES: JESUS' PATIENCE

I love mentoring. I look forward to hanging out with the guys I teach and from whom I learn. Whatever I'm facing in life, mentoring encounters help me regain my focus on the importance of people. That doesn't mean, though, that I never need patience in dealing with those I mentor. Sometimes I'm ready to toss in the towel. That's when I'm glad to have Jesus' example to follow. Jesus' mentees were sometimes quite a challenge. The Gospel of Mark gives us some excellent examples:

- Sometimes the disciples struggled to realize who their mentor was. For instance, when He calmed the sea, they asked, "Who then is this?" (4:35-41).
- They didn't always understand what Jesus could do. They were "utterly astounded" when He not only healed but brought back to life the synagogue leader's 12-year-old daughter (5:30-43).
- They failed to learn from previous miracles. In the Mark 8 account of the feeding of the 4,000, the disciples seemed to have no frame of reference for how Jesus might feed the crowds, though they had already experienced the feeding of the 5,000 recorded in Mark 6 (6:41; 8:1-10).
- These mentees had God's power at their disposal, but they still failed in at least one exorcism—primarily because they lacked faith and prayer (9:14-29).
- These same disciples criticized others who did defeat demons and even argued about which disciple was the greatest in the kingdom (9:33-41).
- They rebuked people for bringing children to their mentor (10:13-16).
- Two of the men dared to ask for the best seats in Jesus' kingdom (10:35-41).
- One of them betrayed Jesus to death (14:43-46).
- All of the disciples deserted Jesus when He was arrested (14:50).
- One of them denied being a mentee at all (14:66-72).

Is this the bunch that you would pick as mentees? Jesus did. Jesus chose these men because He knew what the Father could do through them. He saw in them their potential for leadership in God's kingdom. To put it simply, Jesus called these men to Himself and patiently taught them, believing in faith that the Father was going to mold them to be what He wanted them to be. He chose men who were unknown and untrained. It's obvious that

 One of Jesus' mentees, Judas, was a traitor who never truly turned to Jesus as his Savior. Instead, he became a tool in God's hand to bring about Jesus' necessary death.

it was only in God's power that these men would make a difference. That's part of the fun of mentoring—watching God take people who are powerless and give them power to do mighty things in His name.

Robert Coleman is the author of *The Master Plan of Evangelism*, a study of Jesus' work with His disciples. This book, one of the best-selling books ever written about evangelism, is really about discipleship as much as it is about evangelism. Jesus mentored His disciples so that they would be great evangelists.

What I so respect about Dr. Coleman is that he lives out what he wrote in his book. My colleague, Tim Beougher, was one of Dr. Coleman's mentees years ago. Around the world are other Christian leaders who studied in Dr. Coleman's shadow. To this day, I've never seen him when he didn't have a student traveling with him and learning from this true man of God along the way. To be honest, I wouldn't mind having more opportunities to walk in Dr. Coleman's shadow just to learn from his experiences. I trust that he would be patient with me, believing God to grow me even as I learn as a man more than 50 years old.

Jesus' work with His disciples reminds us that everybody can benefit from mentoring. If you get prideful sometimes, you're like James and John. If you have a tendency to speak too quickly, you're similar to Peter. If you forget God's miracles and take His presence for granted, you could've joined Jesus' disciples. If your faith wavers occasionally, you're one of the crowd. But, there's good news: It's possible that God has planned a divine intersection for you to grow in His grace. God might be sending you the gift of a person in whose shadow you'll stand.

If you desire to be a mentor, don't miss Jesus' example of patience and persistence. Mentoring can be messy, time-consuming, and frustrating, especially if God directs you to mentor someone who has much room for growth. Giving up may seem a lot easier than pressing on. But don't give up. It's God's responsibility to empower and grow those you mentor. At the end of the day, it's your responsibility to simply remain faithful to your task and to do what Jesus did.

 "[Mentoring] will be slow, tedious, painful, and probably unnoticed by people at first, but the end result will be glorious, even if we don't live to see it." –Robert Coleman, *The Master Plan of Evangelism*[3]

THROUGH THE WEEK

> **CONNECT:** The sooner someone has a mentor in his or her life, the better. Find out about opportunities to invest in the life of a child in your community who may not have someone investing in him or her. Check with your local Big Brothers, Big Sisters or the Boys & Girls Club.

> **PRAY:** If you aren't mentoring someone, ask God to begin to direct you to a potential mentee. Also ask God to remind you of the patience He has shown you.

> **READ:** Want to learn about famous disciple-makers? Check out these biographies:

• John Wesley, *ccel.org*
• Henrietta Mears, *isae.wheaton.edu*
• Dawson Trotman, *discipleshiplibrary.com*
• Bill Bright, *isae.wheaton.edu*
• Max Barnett, *discipleshiplibrary.com*

> **STUDY:** As we read this week, prayer is an integral aspect of Jesus' work in modern mentors. Thankfully, Scripture gives us many examples of people talking to God. Read through the following list this week:

• Abraham—Genesis 18
• Moses—Exodus 32 and 33
• Hannah—1 Samuel 2
• Nehemiah—Nehemiah 1
• David—Psalm 51
• Jeremiah—Jeremiah 1
• Daniel—Daniel 6
• Mary—Luke 1
• Jesus—John 17
• Disciples—Luke 11
• Peter—Acts 10
• Paul—Acts 16

3

SESSION THREE

MENTORING IN ACTION :
PAUL & TIMOTHY

I was a young professor attending an international evangelism conference. I knew what mentoring was (or at least I thought I did), but I hadn't thought much about the potential cost of investing in another's life. I certainly wasn't prepared for what the speaker said. His passion inspired me though I'd heard most of the material before—until he spoke more personally about one of his mentors.

Here's my best memory of what he said:

> The doctors discovered I needed a kidney. My mentor was a match, and he provided that kidney. Both of us entered the hospital, and one of his kidneys became mine. When I talk about my mentor investing in me, I really mean that he's in me.

Wow. That moment took my breath away. Sometimes, apparently, mentoring costs you part of yourself.

Mentors come in all shapes and sizes, from the kind you just read about to the occasional mentor who speaks into your life from time to time. Before we study the life of Paul, consider how you'd write a job description for the position of mentor.

What would you include as background requirements for the position? College educated? Married? Single? A teacher? Trustworthy? Successful?

If you had to pick one quality to be the most important for a mentor to have, what would it be and why?

PAUL'S HISTORY: THE BACKGROUND OF A MENTOR?

Paul was a first-century mentor who, seeking to raise up another generation of Christian leaders, invested his life in younger men. We can learn valuable mentoring principles from his story.

....

 You can read the specifics of Paul's story in chapters 13–28 of the Book of Acts and in the letters attributed to him in the New Testament.

First, a little background. Paul was given his Hebrew name "Saul" at birth. He was born to a Jewish family in the city of Tarsus, a port city of Turkey. It's likely that Paul came from a family of tentmakers, the profession he chose for himself prior to his Christian conversion. Paul and his family were Roman citizens, but he grew up in Jerusalem. He was trained in the Jewish religion by a leading Jewish scholar named Gamaliel, and Paul later became a Pharisee, a leader among Jews. He was zealous in his Judaism—so zealous that he thought himself to be "blameless" according to the Law. Some scholars believe Paul was a "Jewish missionary" who worked hard to convert Gentiles to Judaism.

Paul is perhaps better known for persecuting the early Christian church that taught Jesus was the long-awaited Messiah. With the authority and consent of the chief priest, Paul arrested believers, had them imprisoned, and consented to their deaths. He was present when Stephen was martyred and approved of the death (Acts 7:57–8:1). Here's how he described his own past: "I persecuted God's church to an extreme degree and tried to destroy it" (Galatians 1:13). He mistreated men and women (Acts 22:4), punishing them in synagogues and pursuing them even into foreign cities (Acts 26:11).

It was on the road to one of those foreign cities where Paul had a dramatic spiritual encounter. The resurrected Jesus appeared, blinded Paul with a brilliant radiance, and told him to go into the city to receive further instruction. That instruction came from a man named Ananias (Acts 22:1-16).

Ananias was hesitant to speak to Paul, and that's understandable given Paul's destructive history. However, God had already called Paul to be an instrument for carrying God's name to "Gentiles, kings, and the Israelites" (Acts 9:15). It was within the context of that calling that Paul poured his life into the next generation of Christian leaders.

A zealot. A persecutor. A murderer. Did you include any of those characteristics on your job description for a mentor? Surely not. Knowing Paul's biography, I almost laugh when I read one writer's words about mentors: "Keep in mind, mentors are not . . . perfect people."[1] Not even the best mentors come close to perfect. Mentors are often just one step ahead of their disciples. In Paul's case, he had many leadership qualities, but his background was far from what you'd expect.

That's great news for all of us. If perfection or a spiritual pedigree were requirements to be a mentor, none of us would have or be one. Many mentors are good mentors precisely because they've navigated tough situations in their lives. Because they've overcome their own regrettable decisions, they can lead others to do the same. Some of the best mentors I know have a deep appreciation for God's forgiving grace because they've experienced it so deeply. They've conquered their pasts through the power of God.

 A Pharisee was a member of a sect of Jewish religious leaders who emphasized strict observance of Jewish laws and ceremonies. They often had the reputation of thinking themselves more righteous than other Jews.

As you review Paul's "credentials" for mentoring, or lack thereof, how would you say his past failings might have prepared him for the work ahead of him?

The fact that our mentors are human like us means that we must be willing to grant them grace not only for the past, but also in the present and future. If we choose to work with mentors, we let go of our temptation to judge them for pasts that God already forgave. Today, we must accept that our mentors will sin, and we'll probably see it happen. All mentors will let us down at some point. That doesn't mean they have nothing to offer us.

Accepting that our mentors will reveal their human foibles at some point is an important part of setting reasonable expectations for the relationship—hang out with somebody long enough, and you'll see each other's weaknesses. The danger is that we may not know how to respond when the other person isn't perfect.

Michael Card wrote at length about his mentoring relationship with Bill Lane in the book *The Walk*. Dr. Lane and Card met on the campus of Western Kentucky University in Bowling Green, Kentucky. Lane walked the campus regularly talking with male students he was mentoring. Lane and Card walked and talked together throughout most of Card's college years. This led to a 25-year relationship so deep that Card named his oldest son after William Lane. Listen to some wisdom that Card learned from his mentor:

> "A true soul-friend is willing to endure the inevitable pain that is caused by being in a relationship with another human being. 'We are fragile and fallen people,' Bill would say. 'Often we hurt each other.' In a genuine relationship, friends always love and always forgive. A true soul-friend understands this and learns to rely totally on God's grace to make it possible."[2]

It's easier to forgive others when you understand and have accepted God's forgiveness as Paul did. He saw himself as the worst of sinners (1 Timothy 1:15-16), but he was a forgiven sinner.

When someone you're close to disappoints you, how do you forgive them and move forward?

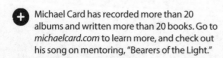

Michael Card has recorded more than 20 albums and written more than 20 books. Go to *michaelcard.com* to learn more, and check out his song on mentoring, "Bearers of the Light."

PAUL'S LIFE: GIVING HIMSELF

Paul invested in several men, including Timothy and Titus—all first-century church leaders. In his mentoring relationship with Timothy, we can compare Paul's approach to mentoring with Jesus' approach.

Paul initiated the mentoring relationship.

We don't know much about the divine intersection that led to Paul's mentoring relationship with Timothy. Paul was traveling through the city of Lystra on his second missionary journey when he announced he wanted Timothy to travel with him (Acts 16:1-5). It's possible that Timothy converted to Christianity during Paul's trip through Lystra on his first missionary journey, but we're not told when Timothy became a believer. We do know that his mother and grandmother were believers who trained young Timothy in the Word of God (Acts 16:1; 2 Timothy 1:3-5; 3:14-17). Timothy's father, a Greek, was likely a non-believer.

Timothy and Paul's mentoring relationship provides a model for us. First, Paul as mentor took the lead in establishing the relationship (you might remember that Jesus took the initiative, too, in calling His disciples). Paul apparently kept his eyes open for believers who showed promise, and Timothy caught his attention. Maybe Paul had heard from church leaders who recognized Timothy's giftedness (1 Timothy 1:18; 4:14). However Paul enlisted Timothy, Paul eventually came to speak of Timothy as a fellow worker in the gospel.

Taking the initiative in mentoring isn't always easy. Jesus was the Son of God. Paul was an apostle extraordinaire. Compared to them, we might struggle with whether we'd be welcomed as potential mentors. How do we take the initiative in recruiting people to mentor?

The answer is simple: Do it humbly. In offering ourselves and our time as mentors, we aren't saying, "I'm a growing Christian, and you're not, so I'd like to show you the way." Nor are we saying, "I have a lot to offer you if you'll let me be your mentor." Instead, we say something as simple and honest as the words below:

> I believe God calls us to learn from and teach others. I don't claim to be perfect, and I have a long way to go in my Christian walk. With that in mind, I'm looking for someone to walk and work together with, so we can both grow in our faith. I'm wondering if you'd be willing to pray about starting a mentoring/discipling relationship with me. If so, I'd be honored to help disciple you as I try to grow myself.

 When Paul wrote 1 and 2 Timothy, which were letters from him to his mentee, Timothy was likely serving as the pastor of the church at Ephesus.

We also see from Paul's role as Timothy's mentor that such a relationship often leads to a deeply committed connection. The general silence in Scripture about Timothy's father suggests he didn't have a strong presence in Timothy's life. Listen to the terms Paul used for Timothy, and you'll see that their relationship developed into a deeply rooted father-son bond:

> "He [Timothy] is my dearly loved and faithful son in the Lord" (1 Corinthians 4:17).

> "Timothy, my true son in the faith" (1 Timothy 1:2)

> "Timothy, my dearly loved son" (2 Timothy 1:2)

> "I [Paul] constantly remember you in my prayers night and day. Remembering your tears, I long to see you so that I may be filled with joy" (2 Timothy 1:3-4).

> "He [Timothy] has served with me in the gospel ministry like a son with a father" (Philippians 2:22).

Paul went so far as to say that no one was as like-minded with him as Timothy was (Philippians 2:19-20). Both men cared for God's people, valued the things of God more than anything, and gave evidence of their faith through holy characters. Both were driven by their desires to obey the Great Commission. They worked together so others would hear the gospel and grow in Christ. Theirs was a divine intersection that must have been difficult to deny.

More than a decade ago, there was a reserved, quiet student in my class who sat near the corner of the classroom. He never raised any questions, nor did he respond to any of my comments. I'm not one who lives by hunches, but I sensed that I needed to invite him to breakfast. We met, talked, prayed, and began a mentoring relationship that continues to this day. In those years, we've debated, rejoiced, traveled, argued, confronted, forgiven, prayed, studied, done carpentry, played, and shared life. Our wives have become good friends. Now I claim my mentee as a son, and his children know me as "Papaw Chuck." I would've missed a lot had I ignored the burden God gave me to seek someone to mentor.

What contemporary family/relationship issues, parallel to Timothy's possible lack of fatherly influence, might make a mentor important in someone's life?

Listen to "Walking" by Mary Mary from the *Mentor* playlist, available for purchase at *threadsmedia.com*.

SESSION THREE MENTOR

How would you describe the best way to invite someone to be your mentee?

Paul recognized Timothy's areas of needed growth.

If mentoring is "a God-given relationship in which one growing Christian encourages and equips another believer to reach his/her potential as a disciple of Christ," the mentor needs to recognize places where the other person needs to grow. Sometimes this recognition comes through formal meetings and direct questioning, but more often it's discovered in the course of doing life together.

When you read Paul's writings, you find hints about Timothy's struggles. It's as if you've read someone else's e-mail reply without seeing the whole thread. Even if you don't know the details of the situation, you could make an educated guess as to what kind of issues may have prompted the e-mail. In that same way, we can review Paul's writings to Timothy to learn something about Timothy.

For example, what do you surmise from these words from Paul: "Let no one despise your youth" (1 Timothy 4:12)? Timothy may have been in his late 20s to mid-30s when Paul wrote these words, but some believers in the church weren't ready to listen to a man this young. Seemingly, Timothy's perceived youth was a problem. Knowing that Timothy would need to work hard to overcome this obstacle, Paul encouraged him to be an example through his speech, conduct, love, faith, and purity.

Also, Timothy apparently battled "youthful passions" (2 Timothy 2:22). The word translated "passions" here refers to sinful desires, though it's not limited to sexual yearnings. These desires might have included useless arguing and impatience. Again, Paul reminded Timothy that he could counter his youthful desires by intentionally being gentle and patient while pursuing righteousness, faith, love, and peace—traits Paul would model before him.

Other writings of Paul suggest that Timothy was a timid person. Paul reminded him that God has not "given us a spirit of fearfulness" (2 Timothy 1:7), and he warned the Corinthians not to create fear in Timothy when he visited their congregation (1 Corinthians 16:10).

Frequent illnesses and stomach problems also haunted Timothy (1 Timothy 5:23). Poor sanitation and contaminated water probably contributed to this issue. Whatever the illnesses were, they were recurrent enough that Paul was aware of them. We can't know for certain, but chronic illness may have tempted Timothy to grow discouraged and frustrated. If so, Paul could have encouraged Timothy with the lessons he learned via his own ever-present "thorn in the flesh" (2 Corinthians 12:7-10).

Young. Lustful. Timid. Often ill. That's the picture of Timothy we find in Paul's writings. Yet Paul not only addressed each issue, he also pushed Timothy to press on in spite of these obstacles. In the power of the Spirit and with the support of his fellow believers, Timothy could grow as a Christian leader. His mentor, Paul, would be beside him.

Where do you need to grow? Have you let your age convince you that God isn't ready to use you yet? Do you wrestle with lust? Does fear keep you from following God completely? Have recurrent struggles caused you to question God's care? Are other unnamed issues hindering your walk with God? Pray for God to send you a mentor who will recognize your areas of needed growth—and who will love you anyway.

Regarding Timothy's traits that might have worked against him as a leader—his youth, his passions, his timidity—how could a mentor help him temper those traits?

Think about a time when someone pointed out a less-than-favorable trait of yours, but in a helpful way. What made their strategy work for you?

Paul invited Timothy into his life.

Not only can we learn about Timothy from Paul's letters, we can also learn about Paul's role as a mentor. It's clear from Paul's writings that he opened his life to Timothy. The Second Letter to Timothy is considered to be Paul's last will and testament—his final words to Timothy as Paul awaited his death in a Roman prison. This letter is emotional, gripping, and personal. Read the verses below, and consider how much Paul shared his life with Timothy.

> **"But you have followed my teaching, conduct, purpose, faith, patience, love, and endurance, along with the persecutions and sufferings that came to me in Antioch, Iconium, and Lystra. What persecutions I endured! Yet the Lord rescued me from them all"** (2 Timothy 3:10-11).

These verses read like a journal, and they're packed with detail. Using nine different nouns, Paul summarized all that Timothy had seen. The first seven aspects are positive, showing that Timothy heard Paul's teaching, saw his obedience, witnessed his faith and persistence, and experienced his love. Young Timothy saw Christ modeled in his mentor in each of the areas listed below:

1. Teaching: the gospel, Paul's message of Christ
2. Conduct: Paul's way of life, actions based on his beliefs
3. Purpose: Paul's single-minded commitment to follow Christ and make Him known
4. Faith: Paul's confidence in God evidenced in his actions
5. Patience: Paul's long-suffering and persistence even when others weren't on board
6. Love: Paul's agape love, loving friends and enemies in deed even when feelings of love weren't present
7. Endurance: Paul's faithfulness amid trying circumstances

But look at the last two nouns in Paul's list: persecutions and sufferings (Acts 13–14). Paul had been driven out of Pisidia, mistreated in Iconium, and stoned in Lystra. Timothy may have even been present when Paul was persecuted and left for dead in Lystra. If so, he saw Paul pay a price for his faith, and yet God preserved Paul for at least a while to preach again.

Timothy also knew of times when Paul was whipped, beaten with rods, confronted with danger on all sides—and still found God's strength ever present in his weakness (2 Corinthians 11:23-30; 12:10). Timothy, who we've learned was timid, would likely need to remember that testimony when he was imprisoned for his faith (Hebrews 13:23). Paul invited Timothy to the thrill of the mountaintops, and he allowed Timothy to help bear his anguish in the valleys. That's sharing life.

 Agape love denotes the special unconditional love of God. This type of love has God as its object, true motivator, and source. [3]

 The word translated *have followed* in verse 10 doesn't refer to a casual observation. It means "to follow closely, to investigate, to observe carefully."

Early in my ministry I had the opportunity to watch someone who, like Paul, knew how to invite people into every part of life. Her name was Shirley. She specialized in single adult ministry and was a model mentor for single women. I connected with Shirley when she invited me to speak at singles conferences she was organizing.

Shirley traveled the world with her husband, who worked for the U.S. government. Wherever she went, she connected with young adults and invited them to minister alongside her. Hundreds of single adults around the world know Jesus better because of Shirley's influence. Today she still continues to spread her witness by training believers to work in prison ministries.

What I most respect about Shirley is her unique ability to invite others into her world in an unassuming way. She's naturally inviting, and others gravitate toward her. I've seen her answer life questions from young women who simply trust her wisdom. My wife and I have watched Shirley model persevering faith after an accident caused her enduring back problems. Shirley's life experiences, both positive and negative, have only strengthened her faith, and many people she has influenced still turn to her for prayer.

Do you have someone who lets you in close enough to see the mountains and the valleys? Do you have a Paul or a Shirley?

How, if any, does the role of a mentor change when a mentee goes through something incredibly difficult?

What answer would you give if someone asked why God didn't rescue you from life's difficulties?

Paul challenged Timothy to fulfill his calling.

The 2008 Summer Olympics 4x100 relay races were disasters for the U.S. men's and women's teams. The problem wasn't that the teams weren't fast. No, the problem was that both teams fumbled baton transfers and never made it past the semifinals. The women dropped the baton, and the men never transferred the baton cleanly. One of the sprinters said later, "By the time I went to grab it, there was nothing."[4] That's heartbreaking, because no matter how fast you can run, you can't win a relay race if you don't pass the baton within the passing zone.

I fear too many might say the same thing about the church's "baton" as leadership is passed from one generation to the next. I have a lot of confidence and hope in the next generation of church leaders. They have a heightened awareness of the importance of doing social justice ministry along with evangelism. In some ways, the reckless, trusting faith of this rising generation of adults puts my generation to shame.

But my concern is that as older church leaders, we're not doing enough to pass the faith on to the next generation. I sometimes wonder if young adult Christians feel as if they're reaching back, and nothing is there. Intergenerational mentoring can correct that problem.

The apostle Paul got it right. He called Timothy to travel with him and learn from him, but he made Timothy do more than observe. Paul knew Timothy was gifted, so much so that the church affirmed him and set him apart for ministry (1 Timothy 4:14). The apostle trained Timothy, sent him out to do ministry, and often reconnected with him between tasks.

A quick review of Timothy's work shows how much Paul trusted him. Timothy accompanied Paul on portions of two of his missionary journeys, and he accepted Paul's assignments on the apostle's behalf. Timothy and Silas stayed in Berea to minister after the crowds ran Paul off (Acts 17:10-15). Later, after the men rejoined Paul in Athens, Paul sent Timothy out again to check on the churches planted in Macedonia (1 Thessalonians 3:1-2). When Paul couldn't go to Corinth, he sent Timothy, his "dearly loved and faithful son in the Lord" (1 Corinthians 4:17).

From prison, Paul sent Timothy to Philippi to get a report on that good church (Philippians 2:19-20). Paul also trusted Timothy to deal with false teachers in the church at Ephesus (1 Timothy 1:3-4). Paul and Timothy were so close, six letters of the New Testament bear their names as coauthors. As we'll see, Paul very much wanted Timothy with him as he faced his impending death.

....

 New Testament letters written by Paul and
Timothy: 1 and 2 Thessalonians, 2 Corinthians,
Philippians, Philemon, and Colossians

Timothy had quite a journey for the almost two decades that he served with Paul—from disciple and traveling partner to and pastor. Paul helped Timothy grow through ministry opportunities and challenges. In our world, that could mean serving as a reference, being aware of opportunities, helping people network, praying for direction, and being available for counsel as needed. Mentors pave the way for their mentees to do what God has called and gifted them to do.

You may not be called to ministry in the same way Timothy was, but a mentor can play the same connecting, encouraging role in your life. Many employers now provide "occasional" mentors or "sponsor mentors" to help new employees navigate internal systems and improve productivity. Some school systems require rookie teachers to work with mentor teachers who have more experience and wisdom to share. Other companies use mentors to challenge long-term employees to move beyond plateau and mediocrity.

These mentors are different from what we've described so far in this study, but they can still have a significant influence. Thank God when He gives you these kinds of mentors, especially if they're believers. Occasional mentors don't typically influence our lives as Paul did Timothy's, but they're part of God's calling us to bigger things.

In your experience, how effective have churches been at passing the spiritual baton to the next generation?

Why might Christian leaders might struggle with passing the baton of spiritual leadership? List a few reasons.

 For a glimpse into mentoring relationships in action, watch the video "Dave, Teddy, and Patrick's Story," available for purchase at *threadsmedia.com*.

PAUL'S DEATH: MODELING FAITH

Remember that "wow" moment I had when the conference speaker spoke about his mentor's gift of a kidney? Let me tell you about another "wow" moment I had when reading Michael Card's *The Walk*. Years after Card graduated from college and began his powerful ministry career, he received a phone call from Bill Lane. Dr. Lane, then living in Seattle while Card lived in Franklin, Tennessee, had been diagnosed with cancer. Card describes the call this way:

> "A few months later, Brenda [Dr. Lane's wife] called and proposed the idea of their moving to Franklin. During the conversation Bill told me why he wanted to spend his last days here. He didn't feel Seattle was home, even after eight years there. Neither did he want to go back to Bowling Green, even though his years there had been some of the happiest of his life. 'I want to come to Franklin,' he said. 'I want to show you how a Christian man dies.' When I hung up the phone from that conversation, I realized through deep sorrow that I had just been given the greatest compliment of my life. There was still more Bill wanted to teach, and for reasons known only to him, he wanted to teach them to me."[5]

When I read these words, I put down my book and just sat for a while with the power of what I'd read. After some thought, though, I realized that the apostle Paul did the same thing for Timothy. As Paul faced his own death, he gave Timothy his final charge (2 Timothy 4:1-8). That charge is both a challenge to Timothy and a testimony of Paul's life. Read the verses below, and imagine Timothy's emotions as he read these words from his mentor.

> "I solemnly charge you before God and Christ Jesus, who is going to judge the living and the dead, and because of His appearing and His kingdom: Proclaim the message; persist in it whether convenient or not; rebuke, correct, and encourage with great patience and teaching. For the time will come when they will not tolerate sound doctrine, but according to their own desires, will multiply teachers for themselves because they have an itch to hear something new. They will turn away from hearing the truth and will turn aside to myths. But as for you, be serious about everything, endure hardship, do the work of an evangelist, fulfill your ministry. For I am already being poured out as a drink offering, and the time for my departure is close. I have fought the good fight, I have finished the race, I have kept the faith. There is reserved for me in the future the crown of righteousness, which the Lord, the righteous Judge, will give me on that day, and not only to me, but to all those who have loved His appearing" (2 Timothy 4:1-8).

The connections between Paul's charge to Timothy and his own personal testimony are clear. Paul knew he'd be facing the Judge of eternity, but he was prepared to do so because he'd fought his fight and finished his race. He wanted Timothy to be found faithful until the end as well. As a prisoner being sacrificed like an offering poured out to God, Paul could, with integrity, call Timothy to that same level of obedience.

The apostle was ready to die, and he wouldn't miss his opportunity to teach Timothy about living and dying. Centuries later, we can learn the same truths. First, daily obedience prepares us for death. Paul could say, "I have fought the good fight," because he had. He knew the power of wearing the full armor of God (Ephesians 6:11). He had preached the Word, even though doing so cost him his physical freedom. Without arrogance, Paul could call others to imitate him as he imitated Christ (1 Corinthians 11:1). *Live like me*, Paul said, *and you will have run the race well.*

Second, we can teach others until the day we die. Just a few months ago, I talked with Ronnie, a member of a church I pastored prior to becoming a seminary professor. I hadn't talked with him for more than 10 years, but my memories were still strong. Ronnie discipled me as his young pastor, and he modeled faith for me. Regardless of what he faced, he always found joy in life. Laughter followed him even where others would only have wept. He was frugal yet giving, wise yet humble, gifted yet trusting. When I talked to him recently, he was losing a battle to a terminal disease, but he made me laugh again. Just a few days before his death, he was still teaching me about joy and trust.

Third, death is easier when someone else is ready to carry on the work of the gospel. All of Paul's work with Timothy was tested after Paul's death. The mentor would no longer be available; Timothy would have to rely on the lessons learned, the example set, and, most importantly, the God to whom his mentor had always directed him. Paul had confidence, though, that God would complete his work in Timothy.

Paul's death was imminent, but he was at peace. His heart was clear. He'd been faithful. The fight was almost over, the race about run. He longed to see Timothy (2 Timothy 4:9-10), but he could rest knowing Timothy was fully prepared and willing to take over the work. Paul's son in the faith would do what he'd challenged him to do:

> **"You, therefore, my son, be strong in the grace that is in Christ Jesus. And what you have heard from me in the presence of many witnesses, commit to faithful men who will be able to teach others also" (2 Timothy 2:1-2).**

Paul's ministry would thus touch generations to come; the witness of the gospel would go on. That's a meaningful way to live and a meaningful way to die.

 Listen to the song "Let it Shine" by Sons and Daughters from the *Mentor* playlist, available for purchase at *threadsmedia.com*.

Paul and Timothy are examples of the wisdom of God's divine intersections. Think about it. Paul had been a murderer. Timothy was timid and sickly. Neither one would've been considered an award-winning candidate by today's standards. But God knew Paul would be an extraordinary mentor and Timothy would be a humble, teachable mentee who himself would then preach the Word.

THROUGH THE WEEK

> **CONNECT:** Take a risk—initiate a conversation with a potential mentee.

> **PRAY:** Ask God to reveal your areas of needed growth to you throughout the week.

> **OBSERVE:** Think about what changes you'd need to make in your life to assure you will someday end well.

> **READ:** Most of the mentoring stories in the Bible are about men. If you want to read more resources about women mentoring, here are some options:

- *Finding a Mentor, Being a Mentor* by Donna Otto
- *Transforming Together* by Ele Parrot
- *Women Leading Women* by Jaye Martin and Terri Stovall
- *The Greatest Mentors in the Bible* by Tim Elmore

> **STUDY:** Is your background a rough one, like Paul's? Look at these images to understand what God does with our sin when He forgives us.

- blots it out—Psalm 51:9
- remembers it no more—Jeremiah 31:34
- separates it from us—Psalm 103:12
- drops it into the depths of the sea—Micah 7:19
- changes it from scarlet to white—Isaiah 1:18

When God forgives us, He paves the way for us to be mentors.

4

SESSION FOUR

TAKING THE FIRST STEPS

My wife, Pam, is a mentor, too. She began mentoring a few young ladies several years ago. Pam learned quickly that her mentees just wanted somebody to talk to and pray with. So, Pam meets her mentees for dinner, or she invites them to our home. They have no fixed agenda or mentoring plan. Together they've celebrated marriages and adoptions, grieved miscarriages and deaths, rejoiced in ministry callings, fixed meals for someone who's been sick or hospitalized, and prayed for each other. I've even seen them do nothing but sit in our family room and talk for hours. This approach works well with this group. The ladies have grown in their faith because of the time they've spent together. Pam tells me they've developed friendships that will last a lifetime.

Mentoring is like that—you just have to learn what works best as a mentor or a mentee.

The goal of this session is to help you know how to play both roles well, starting with being a mentee. The steps that follow outline the way to start as one being mentored and grow toward being a mentor. The steps might not always occur in this order, but they outline a path toward healthy mentoring relationships.

STEP ONE: BE OPEN—ONE SIZE DOESN'T FIT ALL

Writing about mentoring can be complex because there are many kinds of mentors. One book, in fact, lists three types of mentors and eight different mentoring functions within those types.[1] Intensive mentors—the kind of mentor we most often talk about in this study—deliberately and intentionally invest in another life with regularity. Mutual commitment, direction, motivation, and growth are primary goals of the relationship. Jesus and Paul were this kind of mentor.

Occasional mentors are available to help for short periods of time in particular ways, and they complement rather than replace intensive mentors. You'll find an example of occasional mentors on the TV show "What Not to Wear." This reality show follows two fashion experts as they confront and attempt to re-style individuals nominated by their family and friends as poor dressers.

While watching fashion makeovers for an hour isn't my idea of fun, the beginning of the show always grabs my attention. Viewers first learn what the poor dresser typically wears. It's amazing to see what some people wear in public. My point is this: Some of these people really do need a fashion mentor, if you will. That's an occasional mentor.

Passive mentors are role models who give us guidance, even though they often do so from a distance—and probably don't know they're mentors for us. These mentors might be such people as sports heroes, politicians, or well-known pastors. Some passive mentors are even dead, and we learn from them via their writings or biographies. If you know the names of Charles Spurgeon and David Platt, you know two men whom I consider my passive mentors.

Why does it matter that there are different types of mentors? Because we may not always have an intensive mentor. You might look for someone to invest deeply in your life, but not find that person right away. Instead, someone who loves to pray might want to show you how to really talk to God. Somebody else may be available for occasional financial counseling but not for long-term Christian discipleship. If you can't find all that you want in a mentoring relationship, though, don't get discouraged. Thank God

 Learn about the global impact of Charles Spurgeon's and David Platt's ministries at *spurgeon.org* and *disciplemakingintl.org*, respectively.

for the gifts of people He does place in your path, and continue to watch patiently for an intensive mentor. It never hurts to walk in the shadows of several people.

We also may need different types of mentors because no mentor is perfect. No one mentor can give us all the support we need to live an effective Christian life. Every mentor has strengths and weaknesses—weaknesses we can overcome by finding other mentors to help us in those areas. My mentor, Brother Jack, was great at helping me think about God's calling on my life. When I had questions about education, though, he wasn't the best to help. Truth is, he completed graduate school several decades before I was born. Sensible as he was, he encouraged me to find a more recent graduate to help me with those questions. His wisdom and humility were again evident, as he felt no threat from an occasional mentor in my life.

When you think about what kind of spiritual guidance you need, what would you consider the benefits of having several occasional mentors?

Think about the passive mentors in your life. What specific areas of spiritual growth did they help you develop?

STEP TWO: START WITH YOUR FAITH COMMUNITY
You can find a mentor in many places, but the local church is the perfect place to start. The writers of the Bible use dozens of images to describe the church, but one of the most prominent images is the "body of Christ" (Romans 12:4-8; 1 Corinthians 12:12-26; Ephesians 4:15-16). This image is a powerful picture of a church marked by "unity in diversity."

If you think about it, the church is incredible. We come from diverse backgrounds and varied cultures. We're economically, educationally, and vocationally different. Sometimes we're racially and ethnically distinct from each other. Many were raised in church, but others are new to the church world. Seldom do we all read from the same version of the Bible or agree on the fine points of theology. Nevertheless, God somehow takes all of this diversity, unites the believers around Christ, and makes us one body.

We're one, and yet we're different. You might be an ear or an eye in the body, but all of us are in the body according to God's plan (1 Corinthians 12:11,18). Think about the diversity in your own church—different gifts, different strengths. The Spirit puts the church together as He wills, and His plan is always right (1 Corinthians 12:4-12). Within that plan are all kinds of potential mentors.

I'm particularly intrigued by Paul's words about church members who feel less significant:

> **"But even more, those parts of the body that seem to be weaker are necessary. And those parts of the body that we think to be less honorable, we clothe these with greater honor, and our unpresentable parts have a better presentation. But our presentable parts have no need of clothing. Instead, God has put the body together, giving greater honor to the less honorable, so that there would be no division in the body, but that the members would have the same concern for each other"** (1 Corinthians 12:22-25).

It's important to catch what Paul said here: God gives even more attention to the weak and insignificant so that they understand their value in the church. Just as we devote extra time and energy to fix the blotches and blemishes on our bodies, God devotes Himself to those who see themselves as only weak parts of the church. God blends the church together so that the strong help the weak, the older teach the younger, the more presentable give attention to the less presentable, and all rejoice and weep together. To put it another way, God created the church in such a way that He expects us to invest in each another. Mentoring matters.

Where do you think you fit in as a part of the body of Christ?

 Interested in learning more about images of the church in the New Testament? Check out Mark Dever's chapter in *A Theology for the Church* (edited by Daniel Akin, B&H Academic).

Read 1 Corinthians 12:7-21. How would you describe the gifts you have to offer the church?

STEP THREE: TRUST GOD FOR GUIDANCE

We've already learned in this study that both Jesus and Paul initiated relationships with their mentees. That's not to say, however, that mentees should never seek a mentor. God can work that way, using the one being mentored to challenge a potential mentor to give his life to another person.

That's the way it worked in my life with Doug, a student in one of my classes. He showed a unique ability to apply church growth ideas to the real world, and I learned that he was a good, practical thinker. When I saw his name on my calendar, I hoped he was looking for a mentor. I thought I had something to offer to him, and I suspected he could help me better understand the world of young adults.

Doug was humble, yet to the point (as he still is) when he asked the question: "Doc, I completely understand if you can't do this, but I'm wondering if I can meet with you on a regular basis to talk about church, school, marriage, life, and whatever else comes up. Would that be possible?" It was indeed possible, and I was excited about the possibilities. Over the next several years, we walked through changes brought about by marriage, the birth of children, the anguish of a church in conflict, choices in a ministry career, graduation from seminary, and a call to international missions. Today, Doug is serving the Lord faithfully in Southeast Asia.

My relationship with Doug is, in fact, an example of how a mentoring relationship changes. As a student, Doug met with me at least monthly over the course of several years in what was an intensive mentoring connection. Geographical miles eventually changed that, and now I'm an occasional mentor for him. We don't meet regularly, though I do receive his prayer newsletter and pray for him accordingly. Instead, we use Skype or e-mail whenever Doug wants to hang out via cyberspace. The blessing of the Internet makes it possible for a mentor to cast a long shadow.

Trusting God for guidance doesn't mean that you're not involved in the process. Even as you trust God, use these practical steps to help you get started.

Have a wish list.

When looking for a potential mentor, you should be alert for someone who is . . .

• mature but growing
• confrontational but fun
• persistent but patient
• prayerful but confident
• detailed but goal-oriented
• forgiving but demanding
• listening but advising
• encouraging but challenging
• empathetic but teaching
• spiritually strong but dependent on God
• knowledgeable but learning

If you look for somebody who meets all of these qualifications, however, you'll never find a mentor. So, what are the basics you should look for in a mentor? Here are my starting points. First, my mentor must be the same gender so that he'll better understand the issues I face and help protect me from temptations inherent in male-female relationships. The last place I want to invite trouble is in a mentoring relationship. Second, my mentor should be growing in Christ, particularly in areas where I need to grow. His walk with God should both challenge and encourage me.

Third, I want a mentor with whom I share some common interests. If my mentor isn't a friend with whom I enjoy spending time, the mentoring won't last long. I would look for someone with whom I would enjoy talking and taking a walk. Fourth, I want to follow someone who's known for his prayer life. Because I'm well aware of spiritual warfare, I want my mentor to be a prayer warrior on my behalf. I want to know that he knows how to touch heaven.

 Listen to "Running Up Hill" by Us and Our Daughters from the *Mentor* playlist, available for purchase at *threadsmedia.com*.

Fifth, I would seek a man respected by others, yet who exhibits Christian humility. If he has his own mentors he's accountable to, that would be even better. I want to walk in the shadow of a mentor who's still learning from others. Sixth, my mentor should be a positive person, not easily discouraged, one who sees reality for what it is but who also sees what God might be doing in a mentee's life. A good mentor will see in me what I can't see in myself.

Finally, I want a mentor who has time for mentoring. We may not meet every week, but I do want to know that we can meet on a regular schedule. If he's too busy for regular meetings, I need him to be up-front with me about his limitations.

Start fishing in the right ponds.

Start with your local church and see if a staff member would be willing to mentor you. If not, don't be disappointed, as staff members often have full plates. Use the opportunity, though, to ask if your church staff member can suggest someone who might have time to meet with you. When staff members are unavailable, look around for a committed layperson who might be a mentor.

A small group in your local church is another place to look for a mentor. Make sure you're involved in a small group that offers Bible teaching, Christian fellowship, prayer support, and ministry opportunities. That group might be a Sunday School class, a home group, or a men's or women's ministry. Get to know people in that small group and stay alert for prospective mentors.

If there are Christians in your workplace, you might also find a mentor there. Learn to listen, watch, and pray while you're working. Listen for evidence of coworkers who are Christians. Watch how others relate to people and respond to difficulties; look for evidences of a Christian spirit. Pray for God to direct you to others with whom you might have a mentoring relationship.

A sometimes overlooked but valuable option for finding a mentor is your family. In some cases, a mentor can be our Christian mother or father. If you want to surprise your parent, ask him or her to meet with you weekly to show you how to be a faithful man or woman of God. Even if you ask a parent for guidance in only one area of your life, that kind of mentoring can't be matched. Siblings can be great options as well.

The point is that there are all kinds of mentors and all kinds of places to find a mentor. So, do something to get the process started.

What are the first three characteristics that come to mind when you consider what you want in a mentor?

As you review your life, all the "ponds" you fish in, where are you most likely to find the kind of mentor you described in the question above?

Plan your first contact.

I'm an introvert by nature. I enjoy teaching classes, but I don't really enjoy an event that requires me to mingle and talk. I can do it, but it's not easy for me. For the most part, I'm not the person who naturally takes the initiative to start a relationship. Because of that, this point in making contact isn't easy for me to follow. I recognize that there are mentors that want to be asked, but the truth is, making that contact is more difficult for some than others. Nevertheless, sometimes finding a mentor requires you to make the first move.

Dr. Howard Hendricks, a professor at Dallas Theological Seminary, provides some practical ways to make contact with a mentor in his excellent book, *As Iron Sharpens Iron.* Here are a few of his ideas that might work for you:

• Go through the front door—simply contact a potential mentor and ask for an appointment.
• Use a go-between person to set up a meeting. Take advantage of relational networks to spend time with a prospective mentor.
• Recognize a potential mentor for something he or she has done, and ask to learn from

him or her. For example, compliment your Bible study teacher and ask for time to dig more deeply into the topic.

- Offer to serve in a ministry or project to work alongside someone who could be a mentor. Learn from him. Listen to him. Talk to him.
- Open a conversation by asking a prospective mentor about the people who have most influenced his or her life. He or she will likely ask you about the same issue—and you can then talk about mentoring.[2]

Here's a strategy that has worked for me. When I meet a man from whom I'd like to learn, I invite him to breakfast or lunch (it's easier for me to carry on a conversation over a meal). In that first meeting, I thank him for his Christian witness and ask if we could meet monthly for a meal just to talk. We'd have no agenda. No planning. No homework. Just talking. Time together—that's all I ask for.

In some cases, the person has been too busy to meet monthly. Most of the time, though, that first meal has led to some type of mentoring relationship. Sometimes we meet quarterly, sometimes monthly, and on occasion, weekly—but the meal has become a regular meal with several men.

STEP FOUR: DISCUSS YOUR EXPECTATIONS

One of the most common problems in mentoring relationships, as with other ongoing relationships, is unmet expectations. In mentoring relationships, talking about expectations at the start can protect the relationship from hurt feelings and awkwardness later. Here are some expectations worth discussing.

Formal or Informal

The lists below outline the differences between formal and informal mentoring. Most mentoring relationships have elements of both, and both are effective ways to mentor. Indeed, the best mentoring has the informality of a strong relationship coupled with the formality of intentional goals toward spiritual growth. What matters is that both the mentor and the mentee understand the nature of the relationship.

Informal:
- relationships are often spontaneous; "chemistry" is important
- casual, unplanned meetings
- agenda determined by immediate need; any topic is open
- goals often unstated
- often lifelong
- evaluation seldom happens

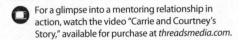
For a glimpse into a mentoring relationship in action, watch the video "Carrie and Courtney's Story," available for purchase at *threadsmedia.com*.

Formal:
- relationships are often arranged, perhaps by a work supervisor or leader
- regular meetings
- set agenda often with intentional teaching
- established goals
- set time duration
- evaluation built in at the end

What I argue for is "goal-oriented informality" that combines both styles. David and I had this kind of relationship. We met every other week to talk about spiritual disciplines, including Bible study, prayer, and Scripture memorization. He also brought a list of questions he wanted to discuss at those meetings. We knew we typically had one hour to cover these details in a formal meeting.

Some of our best times, though, occurred when we traveled together to churches or conferences where I was speaking. We spent the hours in a car or plane talking about God, marriage, missions, and callings. Sometimes we evaluated the conference after I had spoken so that David had the opportunity to help me as well. Occasionally, we just went bowling (I won), played putt-putt golf (I won here, too), or jogged together (David won here, but I think he cheated). Very seldom did we have an agenda, but some of our best life training occurred informally.

Meeting Frequency

Each mentoring relationship is different. My preference is to meet in a formal setting no less than every other week, although some situations can only afford monthly meetings. With the Internet and mobile communications available today, mentors and mentees can still easily keep in touch between scheduled meetings.

When I'm mentoring, my goal is at least two formal meetings and two informal get-togethers each month. The formal meetings are usually 45 to 60 minutes long. The informal times might be as simple as eating lunch, running an errand, watching a ball game, or taking a walk.

This formal/informal combination has always worked well for me. The formal meetings provide an opportunity for the mentee to show his commitment to the relationship. If he always shows up prepared to talk about the issues at hand, I know he's dedicated time and energy to the relationship. At the same time, the informal times are my opportunity to show the mentee that I'm equally committed to the relationship. These casual times are sometimes time-consuming and costly, but I want my mentee to know that I enjoy just "hanging out" apart from our official meeting times. The informal times move us beyond professor/student and help solidify our relationship as Christian brothers and friends.

Every mentor and mentee must decide how often they'll meet, determine the schedule up-front, and strive to meet those expectations.

Your Goals

Tim Elmore, the founder and president of Growing Leaders, Inc., has committed his life to training leaders—especially young leaders. I've found his writings about mentoring to be useful resources. He writes that the goal of a mentor should be to help a mentee do these five things:

1. Discover strengths—find out what he or she does well and strive to make that area even stronger.
2. Develop character—grow morally.
3. Determine focus—narrow his or her concentration to grow deeply in one area (e.g., schooling, career, Christian walk).
4. Discern blind spots—be self-aware with the help of others.
5. Close the gap between potential and performance—become all that he or she can be.[3]

This list may not be comprehensive, but it's a helpful start when thinking about the primary goals of a mentoring relationship. When I first meet with a potential mentee, I invite him to write a description of what he would want our relationship to be if he could design it. In what I call his "the sky's the limit" proposal, I ask him to tell me how often he wants to meet, topics he might want to address, things he might want to do, any concerns he has, and anything else he wants me to know. That proposal is our starting point for determining what the mentoring relationship will look like.

I first compare my mentee's proposal with Elmore's list to see if we'll be covering most things that need to be addressed. Most mentees, for example, don't include "help me see my blind spots" as one of their goals (after all, that's why they're called "blind" spots). Many want to focus on their recognized weaknesses but don't think much about building their strengths. Using the mentee's proposal, Elmore's list, and my schedule and availability, we then work together to set a direction so that both of us share the same expectations.

Assessment Times

A lack of evaluation is one of the weaknesses of most mentoring relationships. Business-people in formal mentoring settings are good at evaluation, but others seldom take time

 Listen to "How He Loves" by John Mark McMillan from the *Mentor* playlist, available for purchase at *threadsmedia.com*.

to evaluate the relationship. Reviews can make for an awkward conversation, and many of us are unpracticed at having those difficult conversations if someone doesn't meet our expectations. The result is a mentoring relationship that isn't as strong as it could be.

I don't think this requires a long, extensive evaluation, however. Instead, I suggest a simple one-on-one verbal evaluation that takes place every six months. Both the mentor and the mentee answer these basic questions:

• In what ways is/isn't this mentoring relationship meeting your expectations?
• In what ways are you a stronger believer because of this mentoring relationship?
• What would you change about the way our relationship is working?
• How might I be a better mentor/mentee?
• Do you want to continue this mentoring relationship?
• If so, what should be our focus during the next six months?

These six questions not only allow you to seek ways to improve the relationship, but they also give each mentoring partner a way out if he or she chooses not to remain. An honest exit is always much better than dropping out without explanation.

What might cause someone to drop out of a mentoring relationship?

What do you consider to be the most important expectations to be discussed between a mentor and mentee?

STEP FIVE: START LOOKING FOR A MENTEE
Mentoring is about reproduction. Multiplication. Growing influence. Making disciples. It's about finding someone like Paul in your life, someone to learn from, so that you can turn

around and teach a Timothy, someone who can learn from you. If you're being mentored and the process stops with you, you'll miss a major point of mentoring: There's no end to the process of reproducing disciples.

If you're looking for someone to mentor, first seek someone who shows an interest in learning and an enthusiasm for Christian growth. Watch for others whose commitment is evident in their attendance and participation in your group. Second, look for mentees who share your Christian values. Be ready to push him or her to become more Christlike in the same way your mentor is pushing you. Third, seek a mentee who's willing to invest in somebody else. Keep the ball rolling by recruiting mentees who understand their responsibility to reproduce themselves.[4]

There's another side to this coin, however. It's always possible that God might want you to mentor someone whose faith is wavering and whose witness is weak. He or she may be on the verge of dropping out of Christian fellowship and desperately need someone to connect with. God may call you to invest in him or her because He has a plan that none of us yet know. The important thing is to make that choice based on God's guidance—not simply a desire to rescue someone, but a desire to *invest* in someone.

Even now, begin asking God to direct you to someone you might mentor. You won't know all you need to know, but mentoring means that you're only one step ahead of your mentee. As long as you're growing in Christ, especially if you have a Paul in your life, you'll have something to give to a younger believer.

Pamela was a great example of this. I met Pamela many years ago in my college days. She was an older student who had returned to college—and to a renewed commitment to God—after a failed relationship and the birth of a child. She had chosen to trust God and remain faithful to Him when anger could've consumed her.

When Pamela told her story, other female college students took note. They listened quietly. Some found the freedom to talk about their own issues. Others wanted to learn what they could about dealing with the wounds of a broken relationship. Though Pamela was still learning how to follow God again, she had something to offer those young women—because of what she learned from her own mistakes. Only a step ahead—that's all that matters.

If you're just getting started in mentoring, think about mentoring someone in one of your particular areas of strength. Maybe you're good at evangelizing; if so, teach somebody else how to do that. If Bible study or prayer comes easy for you, find somebody who can learn from you. Wherever you're growing, turn and teach someone else.

Like Pamela's story, what past mistakes or difficulties do you have that might be tools for mentoring others?

What kinds of changes do you feel you need to make to be more prepared to mentor someone?

STEP SIX: PUT TOGETHER A WRITTEN AGREEMENT

Bill Bright founded the Campus Crusade for Christ ministry. When Bill was a young believer, he wrote and signed a contract with God. He and his wife agreed to follow Christ in "total, absolute, irrevocable surrender."[5] Your mentoring covenant might not carry that magnitude, but your commitment to a mentoring relationship should be no less serious.

Here's a sample mentoring covenant to consider at the beginning of the relationship and to reconsider during each evaluation:

> *As a mentor, I agree to model Christian living, teach God's Word, and pray for my mentees. I will provide accountability while offering guidance in living a holy life. I promise to prioritize our scheduled meetings, and I will seek ways to share life with my mentees. My commitment is to train those I mentor and release them to train others for God's glory.*

> *As a mentee, I commit to attend our meetings, have a teachable spirit, strive for growth in my Christian walk, and be honest in all discussions with my mentor. I will complete all studies as assigned and submit to accountability from my mentor. I commit to praying for my mentor and also for potential mentees that I might lead. My commitment is to learn and then train others for God's glory.*

STEP SEVEN: SET UP A PRAYER TRIAD

It's so basic, you might forget—prayer is essential. God divinely intersects your life with your mentor and mentee. He uses each of you to urge the others toward Christlikeness. Meanwhile, the Enemy stands ready to oppose. We must pray for each other. Pray for yourself. Pray for your Paul. Pray for your Timothy.

THROUGH THE WEEK

> **PRAY:** Find out if you know someone who's already in a mentoring relationship. Pray for that person daily.

> **SERVE:** Talk to a church staff member to learn about opportunities for you to better serve your congregation.

> **CONNECT:** Reach out to a seemingly "insignificant" person in your faith community.

5

SESSION FIVE

DEVELOPING A PLAN OF ACTION

We've all been there: Whether starting a new class, a new diet, or a new year, you lay out a plan to make it happen. Day one goes great. Then day two comes—a little less new. By day three, you're out of your comfort zone. Day four offers a distraction you can't pass up, and by the end of the week you're behind and feeling overwhelmed. That's what happens when we have a good starting plan but no strategy for staying the course.

Mentoring relationships can fall prey to this. We may have a good start—finding a mentor, having a first meeting— but then the process flounders. What seemed exciting at the beginning loses its draw. Without a plan in place for continued growth, meetings become monotonous and draining. Sometimes the relationship simply fades.

That's not the aim, of course. The goal is to make disciples who will teach others who will themselves teach yet another generation of disciples. To get there, however, we need a strategy. Here are some suggestions for developing a lasting mentoring relationship.

PREPARE FOR SPIRITUAL BATTLE

The apostle Paul, mentor to Timothy, Titus, and others, understood the realities of spiritual warfare. He knew Christians wrestle against rulers, authorities, world powers of darkness, and spiritual forces of evil (Ephesians 6:12). This spiritual battle is real, and it's intense.

We see evidence of this spiritual conflict all around us. Churches engage in conflict over trivial things, weakening the church's united witness (see John 17:20-21). The Enemy does all he can to sow seeds of discord among Christians and breed jealousy, bitterness, and internal strife. He knows a divided church has little to offer to an already fractured world. False teaching worms its way in, and God's people are sometimes arrogant and rebellious. As a result, we get distracted from doing the work of the Great Commission (Matthew 28:18-20).

We find evidence of spiritual warfare inside of us too. The Enemy tries to entice us into old behaviors, luring us into patterns of our old lives, our lives before Christ (Ephesians 4:17-32). At times, choosing our way over God's becomes so routine that we think we'll never have spiritual victory. Sometimes we wonder whether our spiritual experience is authentic at all. After influencing us to sin, the Enemy then heaps guilt on us; the tempter quickly becomes the accuser (Revelation 12:10). *God doesn't love you anymore. He'll never use you now*, he says. His strategy often leads to a cycle of defeat and discouragement.

In light of all this, we need to learn how to wear God's armor. In *Discipled Warriors*, I tell the story of Tim, a young believer whose church didn't disciple him.[1] They told him what he needed to do (read the Bible, pray, and be a witness), but they didn't show him how. Nobody taught him how to live victoriously in Christ. As a result, he lived a defeated Christian life—even while his church put him in leadership and teaching positions. Tim's story may sound familiar to many of us.

For undisciplined believers, the Enemy's arrows strike with doubt, discouragement, and loneliness. That's where mentors become critical. Mentors guard their mentees against the Enemy's attacks while teaching their disciples to stand in God's power against Satan. Mentors deflect the Enemy's arrows until their mentees have learned how to fight on their own.

The Enemy can still win temporarily, of course. He knows where you're vulnerable— places your mentor may not be aware of. You'll likely fall in some battles. When that happens, your mentor's job is to help you walk forward again. You should never fight the war alone if you have a mentor by your side. God gives us each other so we can help each other get ready for the battle.

In what ways do you feel the Enemy's attacks?

Who picks you up when you fall?

WEAR GOD'S ARMOR

My father was a volunteer firefighter, and I grew up wanting to be just like him. As a preschooler, I tried my best to wear his boots around the house. It wasn't until I became a volunteer myself, though, that I understood how important that gear really was. Everything from the boots to the helmet is designed to protect firefighters as they wage war against the flames. Firefighting requires months of training to learn how to use the equipment and protective outerwear. Firefighters must trust their gear as they enter burning buildings, and no smart firefighters would work without their equipment.

Our spiritual battle is the same. Paul told us we prepare for this battle by putting on the full armor of God:

> "Finally, be strengthened by the Lord and by His vast strength. Put on the full armor of God so that you can stand against the tactics of the Devil. For our battle is not against flesh and blood, but against the rulers, against the authorities, against the world powers of this darkness, against the spiritual forces of evil in the heavens. This is why you must take up the full armor of God, so that you may be able to resist in the evil day, and having prepared everything, to take your stand. Stand, therefore, with truth like a belt around your waist, righteousness like armor on your chest, and your feet sandaled with readiness for the gospel of peace. In every situation take

 "Be serious! Be alert! Your adversary the Devil is prowling around like a roaring lion, looking for anyone he can devour" (1 Peter 5:8).

the shield of faith, and with it you will be able to extinguish all the flaming arrows of the evil one. Take the helmet of salvation, and the sword of the Spirit, which is God's word. Pray at all times in the Spirit with every prayer and request, and stay alert in this with all perseverance and intercession for all the saints" (Ephesians 6:10-18).

God outfits us for the spiritual battle we're engaged in, but knowing how to use that gear requires training. God's plan is for more mature believers to teach younger believers how to use the equipment and protection He provides. That's New Testament discipleship. That's mentoring.

As you read the following descriptions of the armor of God, keep in mind that it's not separate pieces. It's all connected around God's Word. Remember, too, that training to wear and use God's armor is more than simply teaching a lesson. Effective mentoring requires sharing life. As they walk together, mentors and mentees learn to wear the armor of God every day.

The Belt of Truth

Wearing the belt of truth means knowing the Truth (Jesus), reading the truth (the Scriptures), and living the truth (a life of integrity). All three are essential. I've learned that the very essence of mentoring—walking with someone and helping that person grow spiritually—helps mentors and mentees live in the truth. Why? Being a mentor pushes us to "up our game" in terms of our own spiritual walks. As mentors, we must be on our guard against anything less than truthfulness in our words and lifestyles because we want to be examples. Mentees in turn want to please their mentors. As one friend said it for me, "We live differently when we know others are watching." Being mentees and mentors makes us more conscious of whether or not we're living in the truth.

Part of the stickiness of mentoring relationships is that living by the truth sometimes requires questioning or confrontation. Sometimes we disagree on exactly what the truth is in a situation or what an interpretation of Scripture should be. There are times when both of the mentoring partners have to ask tough questions in order to move ahead. Consider these points as you establish your mentoring relationship so you can both live in the truth:

First, be clear about expectations in this area. As the person being mentored, how vulnerable are you willing to be? Are you open about how you're working out the truth of the Scriptures in your life? How deeply do you let your mentor inquire before you consider it prying?

Second, remember that mentoring relationships function not only to prevent sin but also to promote growth. Talk about proactively engaging in spiritual disciplines as much as you discuss avoiding temptations or identifying sin in each other's lives.

Third, whatever parameters you set for the relationship, determine up-front that you'll both be honest. Any issues you hide are the very ones about which you need the most accountability. If you or your mentor find yourselves covering up, it's time to check in.

Finally, understand that speaking into each other's lives and calling each other deeper into the truth are part of a process. This process requires trust, and instantaneous trust is unrealistic. It develops over time and with experience. So, give it time. Give each other room to be human as you walk together. Ultimately, it's the Holy Spirit's role to convict us of sin, but we can encourage each other to be open to hearing the truth of the Spirit.

The Breastplate of Righteousness

Christians are righteous because God has given us His righteousness (2 Corinthians 5:21). Because of Christ's work on the cross, we're made righteous. At the same time, God calls us to live righteously. That is, we show God's work in our lives by making God-honoring choices. The person who wears the breastplate of righteousness lives according to God's standards.

Scripture clearly shows us we're to help each other live righteously—and the words sound much like mentoring:

> **"Encourage one another and build each other up"** (1 Thessalonians 5:11).

> **"Confess your sins to one another and pray for one another"** (James 5:16).

> **"Let us be concerned about one another in order to promote love and good works"** (Hebrews 10:24).

> **"Brothers, if someone is caught in any wrongdoing, you who are spiritual should restore such a person with a gentle spirit, watching out for yourselves so you also won't be tempted"** (Galatians 6:1).

In mentoring relationships, we hold each other accountable to God's Word, push for holiness, and pick each other up when we fall. This is one area where mentors especially must be willing to be vulnerable. If mentors are unwilling to be held accountable, it's hard for them to hold others accountable. Mutual holiness must be the goal.

 Listen to "We are Beggars at the Foot of God's Door" by The Normals from the *Mentor* playlist, available for purchase at *threadsmedia.com*.

I have accountability partners separate from the people I mentor, but I also give my mentees permission to ask me at any time about my Bible reading, my prayer time, my evangelism, and my personal holiness. If I know they might ask me at any point, I'm forced to strive for faithfulness all the time (instead of just in the 30 minutes before our meeting). Do you have someone who holds you accountable at all times?

One exercise I've found helpful in wearing the breastplate is what I call a "sin pattern analysis." Many of us deal with particular sin issues, and our struggles with those sins often follow a pattern. Sometimes we're more susceptible when we're physically tired. We might be more under attack when we're alone. In some cases, being with the wrong people increases our vulnerability. Maybe we're more under attack at night than during the day or most defenseless when we've not been faithfully reading the Word. When you and your mentor work together to identify these patterns in your life, you're more prepared to wear the breastplate of righteousness.

Describe some factors that you think make most of us fall more easily.

Where are the cracks in your armor, the areas where you need the greatest amount of accountability?

The Shoes of the Gospel of Peace

Several years ago, I was traveling with Travis, one of my mentees. We stopped at a fast food restaurant for a quick hamburger on the way to a conference where I was speaking. A man sitting at the next table unexpectedly began talking to us. "Tell me why, when you tell the truth, things don't always go right," he said.

That was a strange way to start a conversation. We learned that our new friend had just been released from prison, had been honest on all his job applications, and hadn't been hired yet. He was frustrated and hurt.

....

 For a glimpse into a mentoring relationship in action, watch the video "Arliss and Linda's Story," available for purchase at *threadsmedia.com.*

Travis jumped at the opportunity. "Would you mind if I took a few minutes and told you what gives me hope when life is tough?" He then told the story of Jesus while I drew a simple gospel illustration on a napkin. Our friend did not choose to follow Christ right then, but he heard the good news because Travis was prepared.

That's what it means to wear the shoes of the gospel of peace—always ready to share the gospel. Travis was ready not only because he'd been trained in evangelism, but also because one of our mentoring goals was to be alert for opportunities to share Christ. We'd been praying Colossians 4:2-4 for each other, asking God to open doors for us to practice evangelism. Both of us wanted to be faithful that day not only to please God, but also to encourage one another.

That's New Testament mentoring. Ask your mentor and/or mentees to join you in praying for opportunities, clarity, and boldness (Ephesians 6:18-20) to share the gospel.

The Shield of Faith

What do you think of when you think of faith? Is it just believing? Is it trusting? Is it doing something? Paul used the illustration of a shield to help us understand faith. In Paul's day, Roman soldiers covered their shields with leather and soaked them in water to defend against the Enemy's flaming arrows. They were to press forward in war, not allowing the Enemy's attack to hinder their forward progress.

Using that image, Paul called believers to take up the shield of faith, meaning we're to trust the truths and promises of God's Word when the Enemy aims his arrows at us. Faith means we press on regardless of the opposition's ferocity, and that's much easier if we know we're not alone.

Mentors help strengthen our faith by offering the voice of God when the Enemy's voice is loud. We thus learn to hear our mentor's voice in a unique, powerful way. Michael Card describes his response to the voice of his mentor:

> "From that moment, though I barely knew him [Dr. Lane], I experienced something unique about our relationship. My ears seemed to be tuned to his voice. I am, even today, able to recall practically everything he said to me. It was as if God had designed my ears to receive this man's wisdom."[2]

An effective mentor encourages more loudly than the Enemy discourages, strengthens more faithfully than the Enemy weakens, and affirms more clearly than the Enemy condemns. The Enemy's arrows are often lies striking at our self-understanding and ultimately working to diminish our faith. If we accept his lies as truth, the result is a defeated life. Here are some examples:

1. Enemy's message: *God won't forgive you for what you've done.*

   The Word: **"If we confess our sins, He is faithful and righteous to forgive us our sins and to cleanse us from all unrighteousness"** (1 John 1:9).

   Mentor's response: "God forgives you; let's start over again."

2. Enemy's message: *You don't mean anything to anyone.*

   The Word: **"For God loved the world in this way: He gave His One and Only Son, so that everyone who believes in Him will not perish but have eternal life"** (John 3:16).

   Mentor's response: "God really does love you, and I do too."

Ask God to intersect your world with someone who can help you counter the lies of the Enemy. Your victories will enable you, in turn, to help somebody else overcome the same deceptions.

The Helmet of Salvation

Ask most people what Christians mean by the term *salvation*, and I suspect they'd mention eternity in heaven. "Being saved" is probably understood to be more about escaping hell than about living for God today. Salvation does, of course, mean eternity with God, but in the Bible, the idea is much broader than that. "Salvation" in the armor of God passage isn't so much about our final salvation in heaven but about having victory every day through Christ. It's about conquering sin in the present tense.

Living in the "here and now" in our Christian lives means recognizing our identity in Christ, knowing who we are and what we've experienced in Jesus. The Bible gives us great news about who we are:

• Children of God (John 1:12)
• Chosen by God (John 15:16)
• At peace with God (Romans 5:1)
• Free from condemnation (Romans 8:1-2)
• A temple of God, a dwelling place of God's Spirit (1 Corinthians 3:16)
• A member of God's body (1 Corinthians 12:27)

 Listen to "Radiant Sun (Give thanks
to the one)" by Brandon Bee from
the *Mentor* playlist, available for
purchase at *threadsmedia.com*.

- Sealed by God's Spirit (2 Corinthians 1:22)
- Adopted by God (Ephesians 1:4-5)
- Citizens of heaven (Philippians 3:20)
- Rescued, redeemed, and forgiven (Colossians 1:13-14)
- Born of God (1 John 5:1)

This is unbelievable news. We're all sinners, who choose to rebel against God, but God loved us so much He sent His Son to die for us. Through Jesus, we're rebels now redeemed. Sinners now made secure. Liars now loved. Idolaters now intimate with God. God loves us in spite of our history.

But while many of us can talk this language, we still don't live in victory every day. That's where mentors can again make a difference. Mentors remind us every day that we each matter to someone—our mentors—because we first matter to God. Listen to how one mentor describes this responsibility:

> "A spiritual mother [mentor] can't change the fact that a young woman's biological mother constantly criticizes her—but she can help that young woman see that her worth is in her identity as a daughter of the King."[3]

Mentors push us beyond the wounds, failures, and regrets of the past. The Enemy wants to keep us bound in yesterday's bad memories, resurrecting forgiven sins and beating us over the head with them. Good mentors, though, recognize that and constantly remind us of God's forgiving grace. They don't allow us to live in yesterday's wrongs when salvation and today's victories are so powerful. Let your helmet of salvation be present tense.

What messages of the Enemy most hinder your Christian walk?

How might a mentor help you stand firmly against these messages?

The Sword of the Spirit

The Sword of the Spirit is the Word of God—both a defensive and offensive weapon. The Word is truth, and that truth exposes the Enemy's lies. Know the Word's teachings, claim its promises, believe its truths, and resist the devil (James 4:7). He can't stand against God-breathed Scriptures (2 Timothy 3:16).

If the Word of God is so powerful, it's surprising that only 16 percent of church attendees read the Bible daily—and 25 percent of attendees don't read the Bible at all.[4] You probably know the common excuses for not studying the Word (perhaps you've used them at some point): "I don't know where to begin;" "I don't know how to read the Bible;" "there are a lot of concepts and ideas I don't understand;" "sometimes it's boring;" "I'm not sure it's relevant—the Bible was written a long time ago;" "I've tried before, and I didn't get very far;" and "I don't have time."

Look at those excuses, and consider how many a mentor could help with. Mentors can teach us how to interpret and apply the Bible. They can show us why even the mundane stories of the Bible can be exciting and relevant. From mentors we can learn principles of time management so we have time for Bible reading. I've heard many excuses over the years, and I can't find any a mentor couldn't address.

Ask God to give you a mentor to help you read the Word consistently. As a mentor, one strategy I've found effective is to hold myself accountable to my mentees through daily reporting. At the beginning of every year, I adopt an annual reading strategy—usually one that I find through an online search for "Bible reading plans." Each day, I read the passage, study it, pray about it, and send an e-mail report to one of the people I mentor. The report is brief and simple:

- **Text:** John 3
- **Insight gained:** Nicodemus came to Jesus at night. I don't know why he came at night; maybe he just wanted some private time with Jesus. Would I work so hard to be with Jesus?
- **Prayer:** "Lord, make me want to be with Jesus so badly that I'll do whatever it takes to get there."

Writing this report only takes a few minutes, but it helps me stay faithful in my reading. Plus, it provides a journal of Bible reading for later reference.

But there's more to the Sword of the Spirit than reading the Word. The term translated *word* in the phrase "God's word" (v. 17) means not only to know the Word but also to

 For a strong Bible reading program, check out "Read the Bible for Life" at *bhpublishinggroup.com.*

speak it. This is mentoring: Someone teaches us the Word, we obey it, and then we teach it to others. That's what it means to take up the Sword.

Urgent Prayer

Prayer is not a piece of the armor of God, but it's vital to living a strong Christian life. So important was it for Paul, he ended this passage on spiritual warfare with a focus on praying for each other. Notice his words of urgency:

> **"Pray at all times in the Spirit with every prayer and request, and stay alert in this with all perseverance and intercession for all the saints"** (Ephesians 6:18).

Every prayer. Pray at all times in the Spirit. Stay alert. All perseverance. All the saints. Prayer matters.

Yet how often do most of us pray for each other? More specifically, *when* do we pray for each other? In most cases, we don't pray for others until we hear there's some kind of problem. Seldom do we pray for each other just because we're brothers and sisters in Christ fighting a real spiritual battle. Frankly, we usually start praying only after someone's already lost a battle.

In response to this wrong understanding of prayer, we need mentors to teach us to pray as Jesus taught His disciples to pray—proactively and passionately (Matthew 6:5-13).

Prayer is a discipline to learn, and opportunities to practice and model that discipline are everywhere. Think about ways that mentors and mentees can practice prayer. If someone asks for prayer, pray right then. Pray when you hear a siren, see a hearse, or pass a car accident. Pray for churches as you drive or walk past their meeting places. Watch the news, and take time to pray for victims of war or natural disasters. Prayer walk in a neighborhood, quietly praying for anyone you see. Pray for families and nations as you read the newspaper or a news Web site. Praise God in prayer when you hear of families restored, sickness cured, and non-believers saved. Start and end your road trips with prayer. All types of prayer "triggers" can lead you to pray continually throughout the day.

At other times, plan an intentional prayer strategy to focus on others. One of my mentees, Brandon, and I once walked through the streets of New York City just to pray for the people we passed. We talked very little as we walked. Instead, we looked, listened, and interceded. In that famous setting, we saw the world. God had brought people from all over the globe—maybe just so that we could pray for them. Perhaps God intersected all of our lives that day.

BE IN IT FOR THE LONG HAUL

Much of mentoring is about challenging people to do something—to take steps toward growth in some area. The responsibilities of mentors are to guide their mentees, support them in their tasks, and encourage them toward Christian progress. Mentors are what one writer has called "'life ed' instructors"[5] who walk beside the mentee and model Christian truth along the way. This section lists some practical ideas to provide direction for your mentoring sessions. These make great discussion prompts.

Q & A Sessions

Mentoring is about listening and telling—it's an exchange. Sometimes it's good to have intentional Q & A sessions. If you're a mentor, schedule a lunch with your mentee and give him or her permission to ask anything. This approach can be risky for you because you never know what might come up as a question, but it will help you get in touch with what matters to your mentee. Also, fresh topics might come up that you wouldn't have thought of otherwise.

Here are some of the questions I've been asked:

• How did you learn to develop your relationship with your non-Christian dad?
• I don't know how to do a budget. Where do I start?
• How did you know your wife was the one you were supposed to marry?
• What should I do if I want to drop out of seminary?
• How do I know God's will?
• What should my resumé format look like?
• How can I get experience when nobody's hiring people without experience?
• What suggestions do you have for dealing with lust?
• What kind of lawn mower would you recommend?

The list could go on for several pages. Mentees typically love having someone to talk with about real issues, and this strategy makes that possible.

Case Studies

Most mentoring relationships provide enough real-life scenarios that mentors don't need hypothetical situations to discuss. In some situations, though, a case study is an effective means to start dialogue. They're especially helpful in learning to think through different responses to a given situation. They can also be helpful for talking about values and issues that cut so close to the bone that a mentee might be fearful of bringing them up.

Here are two case studies I've used as discussion prompts for conversations about ethics and Christian living:

Case One: You're tired, but you still have two reports to complete for a class you're taking. During your research, you discover that you can order a paper over the Internet for less than $20. You can easily buy a paper, make some adjustments so it sounds like your writing, and turn it in for credit. What do you do?

Case Two: Two months ago, your bank wrongly applied $700 to your account, and you didn't catch it. At this point, you've already spent most of the money. If you point out their mistake, it will be corrected. If you stay quiet, you might not have to pay it back. What do you do?

The great thing about discussion starters like these is you never know the direction the dialogue will head. The values you explore in talking about how to make these decisions can prompt past stories and "why I think this way" accounts, and they often teach us what makes others tick.

Reading Lists

This option should begin with the people being mentored. Ask them what topics they'd like to study, and work with them to create a reading list of books, Web sites, and online journals. A quick Web search may show that the material is already available somewhere. Read through the list together, and discuss as you go.

What reading topics would most interest you?

What three books have been the most powerful in your life?

Interviews

One of my favorite mentoring roles is to facilitate interviews between people I mentor and people from whom they might learn. I've set up 45 to 60 minute interviews with church pastors, CPAs, college deans, school principals, sales managers, physicians, missionaries, writers, politicians, and others. All of these people had more to teach than I did, and my role was only to make the interview possible. I've learned as much as my mentees have! Now, Skype and other technologies make interviews even more possible.

Who would you most want to interview? Why?

How might a mentor help you with an interview?

Road Trips

If feasible, travel together as mentor and mentee. Even short trips can provide opportunities for talking and learning. Time in a car can be some of the most focused, productive mentoring time. It's amazing what you can deal with when your laptop is closed and your cell phone volume is turned down.

I encourage mentors to adopt this rule as much as possible: Don't travel alone. If you always have someone with you, you model practical accountability while also providing opportunities for that person to learn. Take one of the people you mentor on a business trip, and stop at historic sites along the route. Review lessons learned at those sites, asking your mentee to do some research prior to the trip. Set up interviews with church leaders in the area. Plan at least one activity that's just relaxing and fun. Pray as you go.

 For a list of historic sites worth taking a road trip to, check out the National Register of Historic Places at *nps.gov*.

START ON THE WAY TOGETHER

These suggestions are meant to be tools that can help you and your mentor or mentee blend your lives together. The mentoring relationship is more than two people walking parallel paths. It's two people sharing a path and sharing their lives along the way. You can spend time with someone, even studying the Bible, and still be functioning at a head level rather than a heart level. It's not until we share our lives that our interactions become investments in each other and we bond as brothers and sisters in Christ.

Just as essential as the gear that helps us engage in spiritual battle is the camaraderie we develop with our fellow soldiers. As we trust, listen, and learn from each other more, we'll grow together to be more like Jesus.

THROUGH THE WEEK

> STUDY: Begin a solid plan of action for properly suiting up daily in God's armor.

> PRAY: Ask God to show you which pieces of His armor you may be neglecting. Make a strong effort to add those pieces to your daily routine.

> CONNECT: Make a list of the people in your life who wear well the armor of God. Ask them the secret to staying spiritually protected and begin to model this in your own life.

6

SESSION SIX

PREPARING FOR POTHOLES AND POSSIBILITIES

Unfortunately, not every mentoring relationship leads to positive change. My friend mentored a young man who showed great promise to be a Christian leader in the business world. When the young man disconnected from his church, many people grieved. His mentor chased him down and pleaded with him to return—but to no avail. During the writing of this study, the mentee had still not returned to his faith community.

In other cases, the relationship itself just doesn't work. I remember a mentee who sought me out, and I agreed to begin meeting with him. About two months into our meetings, I realized that the relationship wouldn't last long. He missed meetings and always had elaborate excuses. When we did meet, his arrogance frustrated me. He expected attention but wanted no expectations placed on him. We met until our six-month evaluation time, and I chose to end the relationship.

In mentoring, problems like these can be avoided if we're aware of the early warning signs. Let's look at some of those signs as well as the possible life transformation found in mentoring.

POTENTIAL POTHOLES

I've always lived in the Midwest, where winter storms are common. Snow and ice build up on the roads, and the freezing/thawing process produces potholes galore. I've seen holes so large that I thought I'd lose the front end of my car if I didn't stay alert. In fact, my car has needed more than one front-end alignment because of potholes.

I wish the potholes of mentoring were always so obvious. As you start mentoring, be alert for problems that might hinder your progress. Here are a few.

Pothole: Not Establishing Expectations

As I mentioned before, at the outset of a new mentoring relationship, I have my potential mentee write his "the sky's the limit" list of hopes and expectations for the relationship. After that, we negotiate our mutual expectations. I want us both to know up front what we want to accomplish so that we're aiming in the same direction.

Jesus did this with His followers. People knew what He demanded of them before they decided to follow Him. His expectations were heavy but undeniably clear. His followers didn't always understand His teachings, but none of them could say they didn't know what He expected. Listen to a few of His demands.

> **"Then Jesus said to His disciples, 'If anyone wants to come with Me, he must deny himself, take up his cross, and follow Me'" (Matthew 16:24).**

> **"'Follow Me,' Jesus told them, 'and I will make you fish for people!'" (Mark 1:17).**

> **"No, I tell you; but unless you repent, you will all perish as well!" (Luke 13:3).**

"If anyone comes to Me and does not hate his own father and mother, wife and children, brothers and sisters—yes, and even his own life—he cannot be My disciple" (Luke 14:26).

"But Jesus said to him, 'No one who puts his hand to the plow and looks back is fit for the kingdom of God'" (Luke 9:62).

It was clear that Jesus expected a commitment from His followers. In a mentoring relationship, the mutual expectations in the beginning lessen the possibility of somebody being disappointed in the end. I wish I had understood this reality years ago when I was working with a mentee named Mark. He assumed that I would help him find opportunities to work in a church, but I thought his primary goal was to learn about being a good Christian witness in his secular workplace. Somehow, Mark never stated his expectations, and I didn't pick up on signals he may have sent. Our mentoring relationship never achieved what Mark had hoped, but I learned a very valuable lesson from the situation.

How would you describe the difficulties of dealing with unmet expectations in a relationship?

What would be your top three expectations for a productive mentoring relationship?

Pothole: Tutoring Rather Than Mentoring

A tutor's job is to give individual attention toward helping you learn or improve in some area of weakness. A student's role is to listen, ask questions, and learn. Tutoring is information-centered more than life-centered.

Of course, mentoring does sometimes include teaching information. At times the mentee just listens and learns, but a mentor's role isn't simply giving answers. He or she should be helping a mentee figure out an answer. It's the difference in the old adage of giving a hungry man a fish or teaching him how to fish. Teach him how to fish, and he'll get his own meals in the future—and teach others to do the same. Mentoring should lead to independence from the mentor and dependence on God.

 Listen to "Where No One Stands Alone" by Alison Krauss & The Cox Family from the *Mentor* playlist, available for purchase at *threadsmedia.com*.

Learning to mentor rather than tutor means learning to listen well. Good mentors don't jump to the answer; they listen to the one being mentored, respond as needed, and point to solutions. They've learned how to "read" and hear their mentees through good listening practices such as:

- Giving the mentee undivided attention
- Watching body language while listening (for example, fidgeting, avoiding eye contact, nodding)
- Trying not to interrupt when the mentee is speaking
- Asking for clarification if something is unclear
- Summarizing major issues to verify understanding
- Asking for permission before giving advice (for example, say, "You know, I think there's another option. Mind if I tell you about it?")
- Making sure that next steps are clearly understood

Here's an example. One of my mentees, Ben, was ready to prepare his resumé, but he wasn't sure what to include on it. The easiest thing for me to do would've been to tell him exactly what I would look for in a resumé. Because I've learned the hard way not to give all the answers, I first asked Ben what he had already done. He had done very little, so I directed him to several Web sites and books for preparing a resumé. My job was only to recommend resources and review Ben's work. Ben's job was to create the resumé, and he did it well. I would also now trust him to direct others who are preparing resumés.

Are you more comfortable in a tutoring role or a mentoring role? Explain why.

Who is the best listener you know? What makes him/her a good listener?

Pothole: Refusing to Confront

While a mentor needs to listen well, he or she must be willing to confront a mentee if the situation warrants it. To do anything less is uncaring. The Bible demands that we

 "Effective mentors stick with helping, not interfering. They share, they model, they teach; they do not take over someone else's problems unless there is a crisis that requires immediate action." –Gordon Shea, *Mentoring*[1]

be willing to confront each other when our lives are marred by sin. Glance at these Scripture verses, and you can't miss the clear call to accountability and confrontation:

> "If your brother sins against you, go and rebuke him in private. If he listens to you, you have won your brother. But if he won't listen, take one or two more with you, so that by the testimony of two or three witnesses every fact may be established" (Matthew 18:15-16).

> "Brothers, if someone is caught in any wrongdoing, you who are spiritual should restore such a person with a gentle spirit, watching out for yourselves so you also won't be tempted" (Galatians 6:1).

> "Obey your leaders and submit to them, for they keep watch over your souls as those who will give an account, so that they can do this with joy and not with grief, for that would be unprofitable for you" (Hebrews 13:17).

If the Bible is so clear, why don't we confront as needed? Maybe we're concerned that confrontation will cost too much—we might lose a friendship, someone might get angry, we don't want to create a difficult situation for ourselves or anyone else. Many people have never been taught how to confront in a healthy way. Some of us have poor histories with confrontation. We'd rather avoid the possible conflict than go through "that" again.

Not only does avoiding confrontation solve nothing, but it also creates another problem—our own disobedience to the Word that demands we speak the truth in love to others (Ephesians 4:15). Because confrontation is both difficult and necessary, we must "build bridges of relationship that can bear the weight of truth."[2] Mentor and mentee must trust each other—and more specifically, trust God who brought them together in a divine intersection—enough to speak and hear painful truths.

Again, this is why mentoring is so powerful. No one wants to be confronted, but we'd prefer to be confronted by a friend if confrontation is warranted. I'd rather have a friend speak truth to me any day, because I know that person speaks out of love. Mentors who genuinely care will help their mentees face reality, even when it hurts. The wounds of a friend really are trustworthy (Proverbs 27:6).

Can you remember the last time someone confronted you about your spiritual life? What feelings did it stir up in you?

 Listen to "I Will Go With You" by Eric Peters from the *Mentor* playlist, available for purchase at *threadsmedia.com*.

How do you typically respond when confronted?

Pothole: Developing Jealousy

Jealousy is a "monster" that can consume us all. We mentors sometimes struggle with our own egos when mentees surpass us in some area. As much as we want to respond differently, our self-centeredness becomes most apparent when someone we know grows beyond us and is recognized accordingly.

Mentees can also become jealous of one another. The Gospel of Mark tells the story of a distraught father who brought his demon-possessed son to Jesus' disciples (Mark 9:14-37). Under the demon's influence, the boy couldn't speak, foamed at the mouth, and often threw himself into fire or water to destroy himself. From his childhood, he had been in this condition, and nothing was changing. In desperation, the man brought his son to Jesus' disciples. Later, speaking to Jesus, he described the situation this way:

> **"So I asked Your disciples to drive it out, but they couldn't" (Mark 9:18).**

"But they couldn't." God's power was available to them, but they somehow missed it. In the following verses, we learn that the disciples' failure was a product of faithlessness (v. 19) and prayerlessness (v. 29).

Sometime later, Jesus retreated with His disciples and taught them about His coming betrayal, death, and resurrection, but the disciples didn't fully understand what He was teaching (Mark 9:30-32). Even more disconcerting, however, is that in the very next passage, these same disciples were debating over who was the greatest:

> **"When He was in the house, He asked them, 'What were you arguing about on the way?' But they were silent, because on the way they had been arguing with one another about who was the greatest" (Mark 9:34).**

Cast out a demon? They couldn't do it. Comprehend Jesus' teaching about His death? They failed. Understand the nature of Jesus' kingdom? Not yet. Willingly follow Christ's model of service? Not even close. Yet these men were arguing over who was the greatest in a kingdom they didn't even understand.

Later, their pettiness was evident again when they tried to shut down someone else who was exorcising demons simply because he wasn't one of them (Mark 9:38). They also became angry and envious because a mother sought the best seats in God's kingdom for her sons (Matthew 20:20-28). The disciples at times failed in ministry, but that didn't keep them from being jealous and petty.

Let's not kid ourselves, though. We can be the same way. We notice when a mentor or church staff member spends more time with someone else than they do with us. We wonder why they seem to have favorites. The kind of pettiness and jealousy we see among the disciples, we can find among ourselves. And the result is the same for both—anger and broken relationships.

Pothole: Surrendering to Spiritual Letdown

Picture this: A group of guys gathers weekly to hold each other accountable regarding pornography. Their goal is to help each other fight for holiness and please God with their lives. The first week, the men who have failed are broken over their sin. They don't usually cry in public, but they do this night. The second week, they admit their struggles, but are less emotional about them. The third week, they hold back a bit, more concerned about measuring up in the group. Around the fourth week of their accountability, Jeremy admits his failure in a joking manner. The others laugh with him, although uncomfortably. When Pete admits failure, too, the laughing comes a bit easier.

By the tenth week, almost all of the men have admitted falling into sin again. They don't weep now, however, as they confess their wrong. In fact, the men assume that most of them failed during the previous week. They don't say it aloud, but they have given one another permission to fail by their decreasing conviction over their sin.

That's spiritual letdown—dropping your guard about sin so that it becomes easier and easier to give in to temptation. It often occurs in groups, but it also occurs between mentor and mentee. Because confession is difficult and strong relationships are rare, we sometimes let each other off the hook from keeping spiritual commitments. "At least you're doing better than you used to," we say. "Well, I'm not perfect, either, so let's just not worry about it this time." Decreasing sensitivity becomes increasing permission to fail.

In many ways, this same danger is inherent in good mentoring. Mentoring demands sharing "along-the-way" time, and time spent together opens the door to seeing each other's faults. The more time you hang out with a person, the more likely it is you'll see him or her sin in some way. The point is this: Beware of any tendency to spiritual letdown.

 "The true test of relationships is not only how loyal we are when friends fail, but how thrilled we are when they succeed." –John Maxwell, *Mentoring 101*[3]

Pothole: Choosing Not to Multiply

If you read enough works on mentoring, you'll read more than one description of the stages of a mentoring relationship. Most include some kind of assumption that mentoring will lead to the mentee's investing in someone else. Consider the following stages of mentoring:[4]

Definition: relationship is introduced and defined
Development: longest and most productive component of the relationship; growth and development of the mentee
Departure: mentee becomes an equal; mentors someone else

Another way to think of these stages is:

Initiation: getting to know each other; mentee is excited and anxious
Cultivation: mentee grows in confidence and competence
Separation: mentee less dependent on mentor; mentee becomes a colleague
Redefinition: less frequent contact as the formal mentoring relationship changes

Or:

Come and see: first encounter to get to know each other
Come and follow: committing to the expectations of mentoring
Come and surrender: deep commitment to the mentor and the mentor's cause
Come and multiply: mentee now investing in others

Whatever you call it, the final stage of effective mentoring results in a new mentor/mentee relationship. The first-generation mentoring relationship doesn't achieve one of its goals until a second-generation relationship is established. It's a problem when this next generation connection never gets started.

Why doesn't multiplication happen? Sometimes it's because the mentor doesn't want to let go of the mentee relationship. Mentors get affirmed when mentees respect and learn from them. That affirmation is often powerful—so powerful, in fact, that mentors don't want to lose it.

That same thing can be true when mentees feel affirmed because someone gives them attention and time. Sometimes it's more comfortable to stay in the receiving role than it is to take responsibility for training someone else. Receiving attention is almost always easier than giving attention.

....

 For a glimpse into a mentoring relationship in action, watch the video "Jason and Dakota's Story," available for purchase at *threadsmedia.com*.

In other cases, mentees simply haven't been challenged to invest in someone else. They might make the investment if they knew it was an essential part of the process, but their mentors never stated the expectation clearly, didn't encourage them to start the next cycle, or didn't equip them to reach out to someone else.

Sometimes the mentee doesn't want to pay the cost of mentoring. What if he or she fails as a mentor? What if he or she doesn't have the time and sacrifice to give? What if he or she doesn't have the discipline it takes to stay ahead of the next-generation mentee? If any of these situations keep a mentee from becoming a mentor, a significant step in the mentoring process remains missing.

One solution to this problem is for a mentor to talk early in the relationship about this eventual goal. All of us can find someone to mentor in our workplace, university, or church. I encourage my mentees to find that person within the first three months of our mentoring relationship. That way, I can serve as a sounding board and resource person for my mentee as he invests in the next generation.

What are some other hesitations about mentoring that you've experienced that aren't mentioned in the section above?

What kinds of things would (or did) daunt you about becoming a mentor?

POTENTIAL POSSIBILITIES
Though we first discussed the potholes—those challenges that can run us off the road in terms of mentoring—that doesn't mean potholes outweigh possibilities. Being a part of a mentoring relationship is an investment, both in another person and in yourself. Nothing good, no real investment, comes without its costs and challenges. But a good investment also comes with a return. Here are some of the greatest possibilities, or returns on the investment, of mentoring and being mentored.

Possibility: Finding Authentic, Rich Relationships

"Divine intersections" are the supernatural connections God makes, like He did with Paul and Timothy. We may not realize the miracle of this kind of connection when it happens, but this gift of a person changes our lives. It's more than simple similarity or common values. It's something that happens at a deeper level than the words we say to each other. At times these kinds of relationships don't even require words—just the presence of a person who meets us and teaches us.

I've experienced that kind of depth in a few mentoring relationships. Kevin and I have that kind of bond. He and I have driven many miles and hiked many hours through the Kentucky woods—but often with only necessary words between us. Both of us like quiet, and somehow our relationship is strengthened in that silence. It's strange, actually—we have learned to trust each other as brothers in Christ without talking much. There is a comfort in that kind of bond.

With other mentoring relationships, talking is much more the norm. Chris always has questions for me, and he and I have talked into the early hours of the morning many times. I know that when we meet, we're going to enter deep discussions. His questions are often intense, honest inquiries about some issue of life. I'm honored that he trusts me to that level, and I look forward to our time together—but I also know to be prepared for a long Q & A session. That's OK, though, because God has given us this opportunity to walk together.

Like the example of being comfortable in silence together, what are some signs for you that a relationship has gone to a deep, authentic level?

What experiences do you share with people that seem to take the relationships to deeper places?

Possibility: Expanding Your Influence

The movie *Mr. Holland's Opus* is the story of Glenn Holland, a musician who longs to compose his own music. Holland turns to teaching to make extra money, and that teaching becomes his livelihood after his wife gives birth to a deaf son. Thirty years later, the principal of Holland's school ends the music program due to budget cuts. As Holland leaves the building for the last time, he finds students from his many years of teaching who have gathered to sing and play in his honor. A former student speaks about the power of Mr. Holland as a mentor:

> "Mr. Holland had a profound influence on my life and on a lot of lives I know. But I have a feeling that he considers a great part of his own life misspent. Rumor had it he was always working on this symphony of his. And this was going to make him famous, rich, probably both. But Mr. Holland isn't rich and he isn't famous, at least not outside of our little town. So it might be easy for him to think himself a failure. But he would be wrong, because I think that he's achieved a success far beyond riches and fame. Look around you. There is not a life in this room that you have not touched, and each of us is a better person because of you. We are your symphony, Mr. Holland. We are the melodies and the notes of your opus. We are the music of your life."[5]

I find those words powerful and moving—to touch lives is what I want to do. And I want to do this for God's glory so that believers become better followers of Christ. Mentoring gives me that opportunity. In fact, I'm humbled when I think of what God is doing through so many of my mentees. I'm so proud of these men, and so grateful to God for the privilege of mentoring them. They are now:

• a missionary in Asia
• a pastor in Alabama
• a successful manager at Chick-fil-A
• a college administrator in Tennessee
• a missionary in Japan
• an insurance agent in Kentucky
• a church planter in the Pacific Rim
• a pastor in Illinois
• a missionary in Africa
• a church planter in East Asia
• a pastor in Ohio

I think of these men and others, and I thank God for them. And I remember clearly that I've been privileged to mentor them because somebody else first invested in me. Somebody influenced me so that I might influence others.

What names are on your list of mentees (formal and informal) through the years?

In what ways do you feel differently now about mentoring than you did when you were younger?

Possibility: Appreciating and Offering Grace

Nobody's perfect, and everybody will fail somewhere along the way. As a good mentor, you'll anguish over that failure, sometimes more than your mentee will. You'll grieve on your knees when your mentee makes poor choices that lead to trouble.

But—and here's the good news—God is the God of second chances. Think about the story of Simon Peter, one of Jesus' primary mentees (Luke 22:31-61). You might remember that he miserably failed when he denied knowing Jesus. Watch the steps to Peter's collapse in denying Christ:

1. Overconfidence (vv. 31-34)—Peter was overly confident in his own faithfulness to Jesus. In the same way, our confidence can cloud the reality that all of us have the potential to deny Christ before the rooster crows in the morning.
2. Fatigue (vv. 39-46)—Emotional drain, physical weariness, and spiritual confusion caused Peter and the other disciples to sleep when they should've been praying. Prayerlessness is always a step in the wrong direction.
3. Self-reliance (vv. 47-53)—Mistaken confidence in our own power leads to our trying to solve problems in our own way. That's what Peter did when he took out his sword.
4. Recklessness (vv. 54-55)—Peter found himself sitting in the wrong place with the wrong people at the wrong time. There was a reason that happened though—carelessness. Just like Peter, we often find ourselves in the wrong place at the wrong time because we trust in ourselves and let our guard down.
5. Self-protection (vv. 56-60)—Peter, by his words and his actions, denied knowing Jesus three times. He was frightened and defensive; we can find ourselves in similar states every day. In Peter's case, he had left himself spiritually vulnerable, and he fell.

Just as Jesus had warned, the rooster crowed (v. 60). Look closely at the illustration in verse 61: "Then the Lord turned and looked at Peter."

Jesus was under arrest, heading toward a cross. Peter attempted to blend in with the enemies, even verbally denying his commitment to Christ. In the midst of Peter's denials, the Lord Himself turned and looked at Peter. Face to face. Eyeball to eyeball. Heart to heart. Loving Lord to denying disciple. Mentor to mentee. The disciple who had said he would die for his mentor was unwilling to even admit his relationship with Him.

....

 Would you believe that mentoring even affects the brain of the mentee? A study at Case Western Reserve University has shown that positive mentoring causes changes in the area of the brain that processes visual information.

The story doesn't end there, though. On resurrection morning, an angel met the women at the tomb and told them to tell the good news to Jesus' disciples and Peter (Mark 16:7)—as if to say, "Don't forget that Peter is still one of them, too." His fall didn't ultimately break his relationship with Jesus; the Lord whom Peter denied wouldn't deny him. Indeed, Jesus would later affirm Peter as a shepherd set apart to feed His sheep (John 21:15-17). What amazing grace is evident when a fallen fisherman isn't only restored, but is also set apart to lead in God's kingdom.

We get the privilege to offer that same grace to our fallen mentees, too. In mentoring, we have a unique opportunity to model Christ's love—and to receive it.

As you review the five steps to Peter's unfortunate denial, which of these steps threaten your spiritual walk the most?

Describe the difficulties of extending grace to yourself or someone else who has failed in his or her spiritual goals.

Possibility: Getting Blessings and Prayers

To put it simply, mentoring brings a lot of blessings. I could never list all the blessings I've received, but here's a start. As a mentor, I've been blessed with:

• men who pray for me and love me
• Father's Day cards
• "grandchildren" who call me Papaw Chuck
• great pride in mentees who follow the Lord
• watching young men become faithful husbands and loving fathers
• Skype conversations with followers of Christ around the world

As a mentee, I've been blessed with men who are always available when I need advice. They love me, pray for me, and encourage me. When I've struggled, my mentors have stood beside me and prayed me through the battles. They've directed me toward opportunities and challenged me to push myself beyond my level of comfort. All have loved and welcomed my wife. I suspect that I wouldn't be where I am today without my mentors, and they've truly been God's blessings to me.

There is, however, another way that my mentors have blessed me. They've granted me forgiveness when needed, directed me when I've been confused, and loved me when I've messed up. They have shown me grace that I didn't deserve.

As a young child, I learned about grace in a most unexpected way—watching professional wrestling with my grandma. "Rasslin," she called it. Many were the Saturdays when we'd gather around her television to watch her heroes.

Occasionally those heroes became "bad guys" and joined the "villain" teams in the ring. I would've thought that this might disgust my grandma, and we'd stop watching the show. That wasn't what happened, though. Instead, my grandma always believed that her heroes would come back; they'd return to the good side eventually. Just the possibility of their return gave my grandma hope. Lest we miss the fulfillment of her faith, we watched "rasslin" even more until her hero-turned-villain became a "good guy" again.

Grandma always saw the good in her heroes, even when they turned evil. Give them enough time, and they'd come back into the "good guy" fold. "You can't give up on them," she'd say, "good will come out of this."

There have been times in my life when I've needed to hear my grandma's words on my behalf, "You can't give up on him." In those times, God has sent one mentor after another who's never given up on me. It's hard to find that kind of blessing.

Think of someone who has believed in you. How did that person's faith in you impact your life?

What keeps us believing in someone when he or she seems to have fallen off the right path?

A CHALLENGE FOR YOU

I don't know what God has planned for your life. What I do know is that He expects someone to help you grow in your Christian faith. He wants other believers to disciple you, to walk with you along the way today as you become more Christlike.

Maybe God's plan is for you to be the best engineer in the world, or the most knowledgeable physician or nurse. Maybe the most talented singer or musician, or the most gifted teacher in any school. A great salesman. An effective writer. A courageous police officer. Whatever God wants for you, He expects you to grow along the way. A good mentor will help make that happen.

Or, perhaps God is calling you to vocational ministry. Maybe He wants you to be a pastor or a missionary. A denominational leader. A seminary or university professor. A church planter. A worship leader. A church staff member. If God is calling you, He also has someone ready to mentor you. Take heart in that truth.

Somebody's waiting to disciple you along the way. Be patient but persistent as you pray to find this person. Then go, walk alongside him or her, and discover the power of God. Finally, in that power, invest yourself in someone else.

THROUGH THE WEEK

> PRAY: Pray that God will protect your heart and mind from spiritual letdown in your mentoring relationships.

> WATCH: For a challenging and inspiring look at the impact of investing in someone's life, check out the classic film *The Karate Kid*.

> CONNECT: Plan to start meeting with a potential mentor or mentee this month, and begin applying what you've learned through this study.

END NOTES

SESSION 1

1. Chuck Lawless, *Making Disciples through Mentoring: Lessons from Paul and Timothy* (Forest, Virginia, and Elkton, Maryland: Church Growth Institute, 2002), 14.

2. Wayne Grudem, *Systematic Theology: An Introduction to Biblical Doctrine* (Grand Rapids, Michigan: Zondervan, 1994), 746.

3. Portions of this section were first published by Chuck Lawless, "Discipleship 101," 30 October 2007 [cited 16 June 2011]. Available from the Internet: *www.chucklawless.com*.

4. J. D. Greear, "Why Pastors Fall into Moral Sin," 30 September 2010 [cited 24 May 2011]. Available from the Internet: *www.jdgreear.com*.

SESSION 2

1. Craig L. Blomberg, *Matthew, New American Commentary, Vol. 22* (Nashville: Broadman, 1992), 433.

2. Tony Dungy, *The Mentor Leader* (Carol Stream, Illinois: Tyndale, 2010), 93-94.

3. Robert Coleman, *The Master Plan of Evangelism* (Grand Rapids, Michigan: Baker, 1993), Kindle edition, location 235.

SESSION 3

1. Tim Elmore, *Lifegiving Mentors* (Duluth, Georgia: Growing Leaders, Inc., 2008), Kindle edition, location 797.

2. Michael Card, *The Walk: A Moment in Time When Two Lives Intersect* (Nashville, Tennessee: Thomas Nelson, 2000), 46-47.

3. Chad Brand, Charles Draper, Archie England, eds. "Love," *Holman Illustrated Bible Dictionary* (Nashville, Tennessee: Holman Reference, 2003), 1054.

4. Dick Patrick, "Baton Drops Mar U.S. Efforts in Both 4x100 Relays," 22 August 2008 [cited 24 May 2011]. Available from the Internet: *www.usatoday.com*.

5. Card, *The Walk*, 90-91.

SESSION 4

1. Paul D. Stanley and J. Robert Clinton, *Connecting* (Colorado Springs: NavPress, 1992).

2. Howard and William Hendricks, *As Iron Sharpens Iron* (Chicago: Moody, 1995), 88-94.

3. Tim Elmore, *Lifegiving Mentors*, location 1249-1283.

4. Ibid., location 870.

5. Bill and Vonette Bright, "Our Contract with God," 2 March 2002 [cited 15 June 2011]. Available from the Internet: *www.generousgiving.org.*

SESSION 5

1. Chuck Lawless, *Discipled Warriors* (Grand Rapids, Michigan: Kregel, 2002), 43.

2. Card, *The Walk,* 22.

3. Susan Hunt, *Spiritual Mothering* (Wheaton, Illinois: Crossway, 1992), 149.

4. Russ Rankin, "Lack of Bible literacy is spotlighted," *Baptist Press*, 25 April 2011 [cited 15 June 2011]. Available from the Internet: *www.bpnews.net.*

5. Bo Boshers and Judson Poling, *The Be-With Factor: Mentoring Students in Everyday Life* (Grand Rapids, Michigan: Zondervan, 2006), 107.

SESSION 6

1. Gordon F. Shea, *Mentoring* (Boston: Thomson, 2002), 65.

2. Tim Elmore, *Mentoring* (Nashville: Thomas Nelson, 2000), Kindle edition, location 1459.

3. John Maxwell, *Mentoring 101* (Nashville: Thomas Nelson, 2008), Kindle edition, location 670.

4. See Howard and William Hendricks, *As Iron Sharpens Iron*, Kindle edition, location 218-219; W. Brad Johnson and Charles R. Ridley, *The Elements of Mentoring* (New York: Palgrave McMillan, 2004), 126-130; Elmore, *Mentoring*, Kindle edition, location 1022-1067.

5. "*Mr. Holland's Opus* Quotes," 2011 [cited 16 June 2011]. Available from the Internet: *www.quotes.net.*

IN THE BEGINNING...
THERE WAS
JESUS.

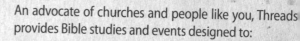

Threads

An advocate of churches and people like you, Threads provides Bible studies and events designed to:

cultivate community We need people we can call when the tire's flat or when we get the promotion. And it's those people—the day-in-day-out people—who we want to walk through life with and learn about God from.

provide depth Kiddie pools are for kids. We're looking to dive in, head first, to all the hard-to-talk-about topics, tough questions, and thought-provoking Scriptures. We think this is a good thing, because we're in process. We're becoming. And who we're becoming isn't shallow.

lift up responsibility We are committed to being responsible—doing the right things like recycling and volunteering. And we're also trying to grow in our understanding of what it means to share the gospel, serve the poor, love our neighbors, tithe, and make wise choices about our time, money, and relationships.

encourage connection We're looking for connection with our church, our community, with somebody who's willing to walk along side us and give us a little advice here and there. We'd like opportunities to pour our lives out for others because we're willing to do that walk-along-side thing for someone else, too. We have a lot to learn from people older and younger than us. From the body of Christ.

We're glad you picked up this study. Please come by and visit us at *threadsmedia.com*.